Simple Solutions to Stubborn School Problems

A 70 in 7 Journey

Dr. Garett Smith &
Dr. Stenette Byrd III

Simple Solutions to Stubborn School Problems: A 70 in 7 Journey

Published by Clovercroft Publishing
Clovercroftpublishing.com

Cover and Interior Design by Queen City Creative

Edited by, and writing contributions from, Robert Irvin

Printed in the United States of America

ISBN: 978-1-968127-33-6 (print)

Contents

THREE
A Cycle of Continuous School Improvement

PROLOGUE

'You Should Probably Wear a Tie'

There I was, minding my business. As usual. The year was 1997. I was 21. New to the district. Green as a crisp dollar bill and eager to change the world—or at least my little corner of it.

This day was our district's summer convocation. I'd just walked into the building with Nupe the Newt, my class pet, in my hands—and a fire in my belly. That's when he said it.

"You should probably wear a tie."

I turned to see a tall, athletic, six-foot, thirty-year-old white man with curly hair who reminded me of David Hasselhoff (of the old *Baywatch* TV series). I paused. Blinked. I didn't know whether to be offended or grateful. I decided not to blow him off in case he had driven KITT to work.

"Excuse me?" I said.

Dr. Garett Smith ("Mr. Smith" at the time) laughed. Not a mocking laugh, but the kind that made you feel like you were in on the joke—even if you didn't get it yet.

"I'm just saying," he said, sticking out his hand. "First impressions matter."

I answered as simply as I could. "Word up, yo. I feel ya."

That was the beginning of a long friendship. We started teaching on the same team. Different trailers, next to each other. I taught math and he taught social studies.

The first rule he taught me?

"We get to work with kids. We should have fun."

And we did. We joked in the hallway, tag-teamed lessons, swapped stories as we planned lessons. Smith had a way of making the work joyful. He reminded me, every day, that teaching was a privilege, not a punishment.

But he didn't just make me laugh. He made me better.

He taught me how to be a good teacher. Not just with pedagogy and pacing guides, but with patience, presence, and love. He showed me how to hold high expectations and deliver soft landings. How to listen to kids when their words didn't match their behavior. How to find the teachable moment even in the mess.

Six years later, as the new principal, Smith hired me as assistant principal. During our leadership journey he taught me how to be a leader—first informally, then when I stepped into administration. He showed me how to build a team, not just a staff.

How to coach instead of control.

How to lead from the middle and lift others up.

And more than all of that, when my twins entered the world, he taught me how to be a father.

I watched him with his own kids, Andrew and Caroline. The way he showed up for them, coached them in sports and life, and the way he listened to their stories like they were the most important stories in the world. The way he spoke about Wendy, his wife, like she was still the girl he fell in love with at age . . . (I'm honestly not sure.)

He taught me how to teach my kids to ride a bike, a lesson that would eventually become one of my most memorable graduation speeches: "You will fall, it will hurt, but you will get back up and try again."

He taught me how to talk to my twins about dating. How to help them choose a glass of wine on the first date: get the second-least-expensive glass so you look like you have some class and don't come across as cheap.

He taught me that real strength is gentle. That wisdom comes in jokes and moments and stories.

Smith passed on more lessons than I can count. At the time, most of them didn't feel like lessons. They were just coffee chats or post-meeting walks or silly stories told while setting up a lab.

But now? Now I carry those lessons like anchors. Like compass points.

I look forward to sharing our leadership journey with you.

This book is filled with those lessons. The lessons I shared with Smith shaped me into the man I am. Lessons that have rippled out to my community, my students, my children.

And it all started with one sentence.

"You should probably wear a tie."

Dr. Stenette Byrd III (SB)

ONE

Kindness Matters

CHAPTER ONE

Trial By Fire: When Tragedy Tests New Leadership

We were longtime educators. But we had never faced tragedy like this.

Dr. Stenette Byrd III and I were fortunate to meet in 1997 when we were both eighth-grade teachers at Jefferson Davis Middle School in Hampton, Virginia. We were both enrolled in school leadership programs, and we used to joke about the possibility of one day working together as an administrative team at the same school.

In 2003 I had the good fortune and opportunity to become principal at Carrollton Elementary School in Isle of Wight County, near Smithfield, Virginia. It just so happened that the assistant principal position was vacant. Dr. Byrd decided to apply, won the job, and our vision for working together had become a reality!

But then an entirely different type of reality hit.

That October, I received my first—and certainly not my last—middle-of-the-night call from a police officer. It jolted me from a fitful sleep. This was before the days of cell phones, and when you received a call from law enforcement at that time of night, you knew it was going to be a gut punch. The officer's steady voice came across the line, and he explained to me in concerned tones that Kyron Butler, a Carrollton third-grader, had been killed.

He had been asleep in his apartment on a school night, simply doing what he was supposed to be doing.

A gang from a neighboring city had driven by and sprayed the apartments where he lived with gunfire. Police told us a bullet had ricocheted off three surfaces before tragically lodging in Kyron's throat. When his mother got home from her late shift at the packing plant, she found that Kyron had suffocated in his own blood.

We attended the church service with family and staff. Dr. Byrd delivered a touching speech to family, friends, and staff in attendance. A few days later, we planted a tree in Kyron's honor and decided we would hold a proper memorial service for him in the spring. Kyron's classroom teacher did an exceptional job of navigating the tragedy while simultaneously bringing her students closer together.

Months passed. The day before the planned service, my head custodian, Mr. Winnegan, and I walked out to look at the tree.

There was no way around it. The tree looked dead.

Dr. Garett Smith (GS)

CHAPTER TWO

The Ceremony and the Realization

We couldn't believe our eyes. I said to our custodian, "Mr. Winnegan, what can we do?" I paused for a moment, then it just came spilling out: "Winnegan, you need to water that tree all day and night. The family is coming tomorrow, and they're bringing a lot of people."

That was really all we *could* do. And then hope for the best.

As the sun was rising the next morning, a few of us went out to meet by the tree. Miraculously, the dogwood was in full bloom . . . and it had a robin's nest in it with two light blue eggs! The nest was just about 4 feet off the ground, the perfect height for a third-grader's eyes.

There was an eerie sense of anticipation in the air. It's always exciting when you have visitors in a school building, but this was for a unique—and yet tragic—circumstance. Our entire third-grade team came outside to take part in the celebration.

They moved in complete silence and settled into their places. There was a tangible feeling that there was going to be something very different about this service.

For months, students had been practicing special songs for the event. Our music teacher organized the third-graders efficiently, almost effortlessly, and the students sang with great emotion. Then the students silently moved back to their places. Some of Kyron's closest friends chose to read poems or tell a special story about their friendship. Tears streamed down the faces of the Butler family, our staff, and students.

And yet, almost miraculously, the family's grieving was somewhat muted. The atmosphere of dignity and respect is one of my most poignant memories from that morning. It was almost like an out-of-body experience. It seemed that, in virtually no time, the final speaker had finished. I think the adults were so in the moment that we were caught a little off guard.

But our third-graders weren't.

I'll never forget what happened next. Without any direction from their teachers or us, 120 8- and 9-year-old children formed a single line in front of Kyron's mother. Quietly, dutifully, each and every one walked by and hugged Kyron's mother as the adults watched in silence.

And that's when it struck me.

Children are inherently kind.

This is something we can build on, I shared with Dr. Byrd. We need to accept this as a fact, make sure our students know it's true, bring it out, recognize it, celebrate it, and make it part of our school culture.

It's right in front of us. Think *inside* the box.

Or maybe we should say: think inside the *person*.

That's where we started to find answers.

– ***GS***

* * * * *

Reflecting on Garett's account, I'm taken back to an experience that forever changed us as educators and friends. More importantly, this was one of the realities of our shared dream of working together when Garett became principal at Carrollton Elementary and I joined him as assistant principal. This first year together brought unimaginable tragedy.

Through the grief, our school community came together to honor Kyron's memory. When the dogwood tree planted in his name bloomed unexpectedly on the day of his memorial, the robin's nest resting in its branches, it felt like a quiet symbol of renewal. But the most powerful moment came when every third-grader formed that line and gave those hugs. It was a pure, instinctive act of kindness that reminded us of something essential: children are naturally compassionate.

That empathy can be the foundation for everything we do in schools.

The moment taught us that student success isn't built only on academics or test scores—it's also shaped by the intangibles: empathy, connection, and the unseen qualities that make a community thrive.

Those are the elements we will focus on beginning with the next chapter.

– ***SB***

CHAPTER THREE

Intangibles Surrounding Student Success

Dr. Byrd assumed the principal role after I (Garett) was appointed to open a new school, Smithfield Middle School, in our division. He and I continued to move through our school leadership careers, always keeping in touch, competing, and sharing our best ideas and practices.

Dr. Byrd's next assignment was principal of Windsor Middle School. Since we were the only two middle school principals in the school division, it was another great opportunity to collaborate.

This is critical: the middle school years are traditionally the time when you "lose" students. They go from elementary school, where they have one main teacher, to a much less supervised existence, where they navigate through several teachers' classes in the course of a day.

Instead of twenty-five students, like a traditional elementary school class, each middle school teacher serves at least 100 students. It's harder for adults to pay close attention. It's easier for students to fall through the cracks.

As former middle school teachers and assistant principals, both Dr. Byrd and I were quite attuned to these problems, and we had ideas to combat them!

We decided that every student in our buildings needed to be connected and engaged, somehow and in some way. Each one. No exceptions.

There were multiple avenues available to us to make this happen. We created after-school intramural sports programs that were open to all. Staff served as coaches.

Frequently the season culminated with a student/staff game. Students were selected to participate in the game based on their play and sportsmanship during the season.

We had scheduling options. Students could be in band or chorus. We had advanced courses in art for those with higher aptitudes and interest in that area. There were multiple Career and Technical Education (CTE) offerings. We had academic teams and competitions.

For some students, we created important school jobs. Select students served as our flag-raisers while working alongside our custodial and office teams. Some worked in the media center for our school librarians as technology specialists, assisting classroom teachers with set-up, operation, and closure. Others assisted our phys ed teachers by setting up for activities at the start of the day and breaking them down at the end.

At times we had to work hard to get creative. I had a program called Courtyard Constables, which helped with order since students were allowed to go outside into an enclosed courtyard after finishing lunch in the cafeteria. The constables could come back inside and report any concerns or potential safety issues to the principals.

A particularly rambunctious group of boys, who sometimes had trouble sitting still during lunch, became our "perimeter security experts." They had badges, with lanyards and everything! Their important job was to check all exterior doors after they finished eating. They were keeping everyone safe, and they did their job every day.

We created a club day each month that we called Enrichment Friday. We shortened our class schedule on those days to allow 90 minutes at the end for students to participate in a club of their choosing. Club options included chess, remote control cars, poetry, music, art, books, walking, running, team sports, board games, and more! We could accommodate pretty much any student or staff request.

The point was, and we made it frequently to students: *everybody* has to participate in *something* extra.

Without student buy-in, the task of schooling becomes much more difficult and less enjoyable for all stakeholders. But when students are engaged in their school, they are more likely to experience academic and overall success.

The middle school years are the most critical time to impart this knowledge to students. To ensure that both students and staff clearly understood our expectations, there were behaviors we needed to engage in as school principals. A powerful tool: making positive phone calls to the families of students, and we did these for all kinds of reasons. But the one principal behavior that put it over the top, and it will return as a theme later in this book, was the emphasis on frequent classroom visits to speak with students directly.

While the students' teachers were listening.

Why? Because students get to hear from their administrators directly and in person. It's an opportunity for them to ask questions or seek clarification.

Because teachers know that the same standard is being shared in every classroom across the school.

High expectations give staff a theme to hold onto. I can't tell you how many times I walked past a classroom and heard a teacher say, "You all heard what Dr. Smith said when he visited yesterday."

I remember repeating the same messages in faculty meetings to staff: *it takes all of us. If a student walks from one side of the building to the other, they should be hearing the same message from every adult they encounter.*

A student who may have not fared well in another school has a better chance to be successful in this type of environment.

We're trying to hire and retain the best possible staff for our students. Really good teachers are high achievers. High achievers are competitive people. Competitive people will inevitably have conflicts. It's natural. It's going to happen. The important thing is to agree on how we will handle these conflicts when they do happen.

When things get tough, we don't fall apart. We come together.
From the simple act of focusing on these intangibles through our school programming, both schools experienced improved student discipline, attendance, and student achievement.

I wasn't sure exactly how much all this meant to staff until some of my middle school teachers surprised me by showing up in June 2025 at my retirement banquet—thirteen years after I had moved on from being their principal. Our local education reporter was interested in why they came and what they had to say.

Here are some excerpts from the newspaper article that came out two days later:

Standing in the lobby of Staunton City Hall June 9, Yann Pirrone reflected on his working relationship with Staunton City Schools Superintendent Garett Smith, calling him the fairest man he had ever known.

At the time Pirrone worked with him, Smith was the principal at Smithfield Middle School in Isle of Wight County, where Smith had opened the school in 2005. Pirrone made the trip to Staunton along with three other colleagues from Isle of Wight to help honor Smith, who is retiring June 30.

* * *

"He was a teachers' principal," said Bill Constant. "He took care of his staff. He went above to take care of the kids. He told us every day: 'Take care of the kids, and everything will work out.'"

Constant and his wife Jane made the trip from Smithfield, about three and a half hours from Staunton. Milton Kemp made the trip from Hatteras Island in North Carolina. Pirrone had the shortest trip, now living in Nellysford. They didn't mind the drive, though, wanting to take part in the celebration for a former principal they loved.

* * *

"He knew every student's name," Pirrone said. "He could talk to them. He could talk to kids about sports or any other subject."

* * *

Jane Constant followed Smith from Carrollton Elementary School to Smithfield Middle.

"He let us do the teaching," she said. "He was like a wall. He protected us from all of the administration, the central office who wanted to come tell him what to do. He would always say, 'This is what needs to be done for the children.'"

Pirrone agreed, saying Smith shielded the staff from everything outside of the school building so they could focus on their jobs.

In the same article, school board members and others reinforced these notions.

Members of the Staunton School Board also spoke about Smith at the June 9 meeting.

Joann Jeter told Smith that he led the division by making connections with everyone in the system.

"This is, of course, a strategic way to lead," Jeter said. "But it is so remarkable here because, for you, it is authentic. Among other things like staff satisfaction, shrinking gaps, and high graduation rates, the result was that students looked forward to seeing you and making you and themselves proud. Each of us needs a champion, and you were that for so many."

After the school board members spoke, the public was invited to [share] about Smith.

Susan Venable, the wife of former school board chairman Ken Venable, told . . . about when her husband was on the board and got quite sick. The second person she called was Smith, to let him know [her husband] wouldn't be at a meeting.

"Dr. Smith was just like a family member," she said. "He jumped right on it. He went to see Ken (at the hospital). He came to our house and picked up some things to take to Ken. It was a very, very trying time because it was pretty touch-and-go for Ken there for a little bit."

Venable said it would have been easy for Smith to just say that he hoped Ken got better, and from there go on about his own life. He didn't do that.

"You took it very personal, and that was very personal to me," she said. "I just want to thank you for that. And thank you for taking care of my husband the entire time he was on the school board. You had his back, and I had his back as well. Thank you for that."

> — *"Staunton Superintendent Garett Smith celebrated by school board as he prepares to retire," Patrick Hite,* Staunton News Leader, June 11, 2025, *https://www.newsleader.com*

—GS

* * * * *

Over at Windsor Middle School, where I (Dr. Byrd) served as principal, we implemented many of the same initiatives and philosophies described in this chapter. We believed deeply that every child needed to feel seen, valued, and connected to their school in some meaningful way. For those students who required additional attention or support, we intentionally found ways to involve them, just like Dr. Smith did at Smithfield Middle School. We gave them important jobs that not only kept them engaged but also built their sense of responsibility and belonging. Some students worked in the office or library; others assisted teachers, helped with morning announcements, or took part in maintaining school spaces. These roles gave students a sense of purpose and reminded them that they were an essential part of the school's success.

Over time we began to notice clear connections between student involvement and improved outcomes in attendance, achievement, and overall school identification, developing that sense of pride and belonging that keeps students connected even through challenging times. This realization inspired me to pursue my doctoral dissertation on the impact of extracurricular activities on middle school students' attendance, academic performance, and identification with school. The research confirmed what we were seeing every day in our halls: when students are engaged in something beyond their core classes—whether it's athletics, the arts, clubs, leadership roles, or service opportunities—they are more likely to come to school, try harder, and see themselves as integral members of the school community.

That understanding evolved into a clear schoolwide commitment in which every student must be involved in at least one activity beyond academics. We made it our mission to find a place for every child. Some were athletes, some were artists, some were helpers, and some found their niche in new clubs or student-led initiatives they helped create.

The goal wasn't just participation; it was connection. We wanted every student to know there was a space for them, that their presence mattered, and that they had something unique to contribute to our collective success.

This philosophy became a defining feature of Windsor Middle School's culture and the culture of every organization that Dr. Smith and I would have the privilege of leading. It changed how we approached scheduling, how we supported staff, and how we talked about student success. We learned that academic excellence is built on emotional connection, and that the true measure of a school is not just test scores or grades, but how many students can say, with confidence, "I belong here."

—SB

CHAPTER FOUR

A Community Divided

In 2017 I (Dr. Smith) had the opportunity to take the position of superintendent for Staunton City Schools. I learned throughout the recruitment process that there were unique challenges in Staunton, including unaccredited schools, a high school name controversy, teacher turnover, and a generally less-than-stellar school climate. This last one was according to the annual school climate report required by the state.

Nevertheless, we moved forward with the work in all of these challenging areas. Our system of continuous school improvement was already starting to pay dividends in the first few years. I believed that getting some quick wins with student achievement would boost staff morale, and, hopefully, encourage teachers to stay with our school division.

But there were still plenty of issues. Here is a more in-depth example of one of the recurring problems.

When I arrived, the name of the high school was a deeply divisive issue in our community. During the 2016-2017 school year, two highly publicized incidents, just months apart, had taken place in the school division.

On Halloween at our high school, the principal dressed up as presidential candidate Donald Trump. His secretary dressed up as presidential candidate Hillary Clinton, but in prison garb. A photo of them at school that day went viral.

The following January in our middle school, a teacher used a skit to teach about the Louisiana Purchase. The problem was that she selected only black students to play the parts of slaves. When a student reported this to his parents, the unrest in the community only intensified.

Parent and citizen groups began to form as a result of this negative publicity, and, unfortunately, they became stories on a national level.

There's no question our students felt the disequilibrium in our community, and this was reflected in their behavior toward each other in school. Particularly, in my opinion, when it came to race relations.

When I arrived, the name of the high school was Robert E. Lee High School. Its mascots for team sports were the "Fighting Leemen" for boys and the "Lee Ladies" for girls. For our daughter, who moved with us from Newport News to start her junior year at Robert E. Lee High School, it was quite a culture shock.

The school was originally named Staunton High School. The name was changed to Robert E. Lee High School, in 1914, when the school board faced pressure from the United Daughters of the Confederacy.

The irony was that Robert E. Lee High School was one of only two city high schools in the area. Like most city schools, ours were far more diverse than those in the surrounding county. In short, the Lee name was offensive to many students and families.

I started on July 1, 2017. Six weeks later, on August 12, the Unite the Right rally happened just across the mountains in Charlottesville. Our city manager called an emergency meeting that included the police chief, fire chief, school superintendent, schools communications manager, the city/school board attorney, and several other city leaders. The question posed to all of us by our city manager: how can we prevent something like what just happened in Charlottesville from taking place right here in Staunton?

There's no question the August 12 incident ratcheted up the emotion and pressure. In Staunton, signs started to pop up in yards and at businesses. One side had a blue sign that said "Save the Name." (Blue was one of the school colors.) These folks were largely graduates of Lee High School, and they were known by some as "From Heres."

The other side had a red sign that said " … But the Name Hurts." Some were local Stauntonians, but many were referred to by the other side as "Come Heres." The discussions at school board meetings were intense; emotionally charged speakers on both sides of the issue let their feelings be known. It was standing room only on those second Mondays each month.

The school division retained the expert help of the Virginia Center of Inclusive Communities, based in Richmond, to help navigate the controversy. A year-long study took place, and it included professional development, public listening sessions, small focus groups, and surveys.

The school board was required at times to hold their meetings in larger venues due to the increased attendance and charged atmosphere. The local police department became a regular presence at school board meetings.

In the spring of 2017, a school board election took place. All four candidates for open seats who pledged to change the name of the high school were elected.

In November 2018, the newly constituted school board held a meeting in a large gym that was part of the city parks and recreation department. Plainclothes police officers were seated inside the meeting. Uniformed police officers were stationed outside or patrolled the parking lot.

All of our cars were parked near an exit so we could be escorted safely out of the park following the meeting. That night the school board voted 4-2 to change the name.

A month later, the same board voted 6-0 to restore the name to Staunton High School.

But in a larger sense, the votes did nothing to calm the waters at that time.

There were too many fights happening in the schools, and there were too many instances of students directing profanity toward teachers and staff. I wanted to be hands-on in my approach. I decided I would meet with the families of any students who got in trouble for engaging in these behaviors in school.

I wanted to make sure families understood what we were trying to do and why we were trying to do it. Parents/guardians who didn't show up to meet with me put themselves at risk of being banned from school property. The meetings were a mixed bag, and after two years I realized that my data was trending in the *wrong* direction. The longer I continued with this model, I was actually having *more* meetings with families.

It hadn't worked.

I had no choice: I went back to the drawing board.

—GS

CHAPTER FIVE

COVID Conundrum

Then, in the early spring of 2020, the COVID-19 pandemic hit us all. We had already been concerned about some of the in-school behaviors we were having trouble extinguishing. But as far as negatively affecting the mental health and well-being of our students, nothing was more devastating than the COVID-19 pandemic.

When the school closure was first announced by the Virginia Governor, we assumed it might be for a week or two, until we could get cleaning and distancing protocols in place. But more and more states were also deciding to shut down, and a quick return to school looked less and less promising.

Finally, we were devastated to receive the news that our school year was over. Schools would be shuttered until further notice.

We began to prepare our staff for a return to virtual learning. Staff stayed connected throughout the summer while enhancing their technological and virtual teaching skills.

We were hopeful that the summer would take care of the pandemic, because people would naturally be outside for longer periods of time. But the number of cases only continued to increase. The Centers for Disease Control and Prevention (CDC) and the Virginia Department of Health (VDH) issued new guidelines on what seemed like a weekly basis. It was almost impossible to keep up.

In an October 2020 board meeting, I pushed our school board for a return to at least a hybrid model so we could start bringing back students for in-person learning at least part of the time. But the board had heard from staff and families who were fearful to come back, and I lost the vote that evening in crushing fashion, 5 to 1.

And yet, at the same time, other families and students were begging us to reopen the schools. Daily, we heard about the strain on everybody's mental health. We informed our school board, staff, and the public—basically, anyone who would listen—that the transition back to in-person learning was going to be hard on everyone.

Finally, in January 2021, we returned to a hybrid teaching model. Class sizes were necessarily small to comply with distancing protocols, and, aside from having to wear masks, it felt like were moving in the right direction.

By the fall of 2021, all of our students were back in buildings, and yet things were even worse than we had predicted! The students were nervous, unsure of themselves, and angry. Arguments and fights were frequent.

It was like nothing we had ever seen. Students insisted on wearing hats and hoods or letting their hair cover their faces. Getting them to engage with their teachers, each other, or their learning seemed almost impossible.

Some days we didn't have enough bus drivers, or school nutrition workers, or instructional staff! But we did our best to hold it together. It felt like we were using kite string, chewing gum, duct tape, paper clips, rubber bands, and anything else we had. Still, staff persevered and families did their best to support us.

There were destructive TikTok challenges that were truly beyond belief, and these made it even more difficult to maintain health and safety protocols.

One TikTok challenge encouraged students to vandalize and destroy school property, particularly in bathrooms, where there was far less adult supervision. Another called for students to insert paper clips or other metal objects into their laptops and Chromebooks to start an electrical fire and destroy their learning devices. The topper (thanks, TikTok) incited students to physically assault their teachers.

Wow. Like an old coach with new players, it seemed we were going to need to start all over—from scratch.

—GS

CHAPTER SIX

The Kindness Challenge

We decided that instead of talking to students about things they shouldn't be saying and doing, we needed to break it all the way down to modeling for them, and practicing, kindness. We needed to be extremely explicit in our communications.

We decided to call it The Kindness Challenge.

In highly polarized times, The Kindness Challenge had no political implications.

Who could argue with being kind? So in December 2021 we started an ongoing campaign designed to spread goodwill in our schools and community. We created a kindness video to kick things off.

At first, the staff was skeptical. For secondary teachers, it was "too elementary." At the high school level, as you might imagine, it was an even tougher sell.

As school leaders, though, once we've determined a course of action in a crisis situation, we must stick with it. Dr. Byrd and I had already had the revelation that students were inherently kind (chapters 1 and 2). Now we just had to convince others. And the only way to change people's outlooks and opinions is by providing them with different experiences.

So we made our decision clear: we were moving forward with cultivating kindness in our school culture no matter what anybody said. We knew it would work.

And it started to; we began to see effects. Families reported that their children were even treating their siblings with kindness at home! The parents knew more than anyone how much a shot of kindness was needed!

Even our high school students started to buy in. At a basketball game one night, our student section was getting a little too rowdy. Our high school principal approached them in the bleachers and reminded them about expectations. Then he smiled and said, "Remember, kindness matters."

Minutes later, the student section erupted in a chant of "Kindness Matters!"

On another occasion, I was standing in the lobby of our high school after visiting some classrooms. I heard the Happy Birthday song from around the corner. When I turned, I saw thirty high school boys serenading their phys ed teacher, who is also our football and wrestling coach.

He turned to me with a big smile and shrugged. "They know it's my birthday tomorrow, and I'm going to be out, so they're getting me today."

Teenage boys singing to their beloved teacher and coach. And totally unprompted in doing so.

Those kinds of things don't just happen. But those kinds of things are the result of an intentional, dogged approach.

Our kindness campaign is still going strong today. Each month, on a Friday, we host a Kindness Day and recognize

Kindness Ambassadors in each of our schools—both students and adults.

The student ambassadors are nominated by their peers, teachers, or administrators. The adult ambassadors are nominated by their peers, students, or administrators. The daily acts of kindness described in the submissions are truly uplifting and inspiring.

I loved being able to visit classes to announce the winners. And honestly, it was a great opportunity to ham it up a little.

We talked about kindness and why we reward it. And then I would tell them: "Believe it or not, we have a kindness ambassador in this very classroom . . . at this very moment. Would you like me to tell you who it is?"

Invariably, students are able to call out their classmate's name before I can even say it. They know! They know who's kind, and they know that their kindness ambassador deserves the recognition.

Staff and secondary student ambassadors receive a Kindness Matters hoodie, and these hoodies have become a hot ticket across town.

The younger students receive a free ice cream coupon, stickers, pencils, and a pencil pouch with the Kindness Matters message.

As we continue to teach students to spread kindness in our community, we've collected food, pet supplies, and monetary donations for local organizations. As you might imagine, it gets competitive.

The winning school in these competitions gets a monetary bonus that principals can use for staff morale, and the student body gets to choose which local charitable organization to support.

A giant metal "KIND" sign is moved from school to school to signal the winners.

It turns out kindness is not only inherent. It's contagious.

Recently, I dropped my car at the mechanic near my office. The walk back takes you along a creek and then under a railroad overpass. The tunnel walls along this underpass are a favorite spot for graffiti artists. Imagine my surprise when I came across this spray-painted image.

The graffiti message I stumbled on under a local railroad tunnel underpass. – Garett Smith

Even our local graffiti artists have caught the kindness fever!

So as we all work to build a healthy culture in our schools, don't forget to think inside the box. Or, perhaps, think *inside* your students. What's right before our eyes that we can tap into immediately?

Kindness. It's inherent. It's free. It's contagious. It's not political. And most of all? It matters.

—SB and GS

CHAPTER SEVEN

Full Circle

For the 2024-2025 school year, we decided not to introduce The Kindness Challenge until November. This was due to a number of new initiatives being rolled out by the state, including new reading and math standards, a new accountability system, and a new literacy act. But looking back over our yearlong data, it's obvious that we experienced a significant decrease in the number of discipline incidents once the challenge was reintroduced.

Students, staff, and families really came together. Our athletic, arts, and academic teams were experiencing tremendous success, and we had strong community support at all of our school events. Our kindergarten through second-grade reading scores were among the best in the state. It really felt so good that I began to think it might be the right time for me to retire and move on to the next chapter of my life.

Once that thought hit me, I could not get it out of my head. I still loved my job and felt energized to work with our students and staff every morning when I hopped out of bed.

But something kept telling me the time for this move was right.

I finally announced my intention to retire on a Friday afternoon in February, and the emotional response was overwhelming. Still, I was determined to stay in the moment every day and do the best I could until my last day. People would ask me, "Are you counting down the days?" I insisted I was not. "I'm still in the game, every day," I said. In the back of my mind, though, I kept thinking about the last high school graduation I would experience with our school community.

It was already an emotional event every year anyway . . . but now, my last one?

The days kept falling off the calendar. I spent the Friday before graduation practicing for the ceremony with our seniors and cheering them on during our annual Senior Walks through the elementary and middle schools in their graduation gowns. Then, finally, the big day arrived.

You could feel the positive energy in the high school auditorium that morning. Our senior class had really endeared themselves to our staff, their classmates, and our community. Our salutatorian decided to call out the names of every staff member who had helped her along the way, adding that she would be the first in her family to graduate from college. She even mentioned the honor of she and me being able to share this final event together.

The valedictorian also mentioned me by name, and she held up a Kindness Matters yard sign at the end of her speech. The class president announced that the class was giving me a plaque to honor my service, and the school placed a Kindness

Matters bench with a similar plaque on it in the front of the school.

The class president informed me that I didn't need to make a speech, but I wanted to show my gratitude to everyone. So I took the microphone and used a line that I often used with staff when I was a principal: "What we have created here only means one thing: when a community of adults is united in the best interests of our children and young people, we cannot be defeated. Let me say that one more time . . . "

Students crossed the stage one by one, and their families and friends cheered for each as their names were called. When it was over, the principal announced it was time for the students to flip their tassels from one side to the other. When I turned to watch, I was amazed at the number of students who had tears streaming down their faces.

We prepared for the recessional. We knew the drill. We had just practiced it the day before. But when I looked to my left, to where the principal was still standing by the podium, something very familiar was happening. With no direction from any adults, our seniors had formed a single line, and each and every one was hugging their principal as they walked by her. Every one, without exception.

That's when it struck me that my journey had come full circle.

—GS

* * * * *

Looking back on the experiences shared in *Section One: Kindness Matters,* we realize that those moments aren't just stories about leading through crisis or promoting kindness, they were the lessons that shaped our understanding of what students truly need. Each chapter represented an important step in learning how compassion, consistency, and connection could transform a school community. But even with a culture built on kindness, there remains a persistent question: how do we turn that compassion into action that ensures every student succeeds?

That question led us to part 2 of this book: the creation of a plan that made success intentional, not accidental. *Section Two: ABC Student Success Plans* explains how we moved from nurturing hearts to developing systems that supported every learner, every day, through a focus on Attendance, Behavior, and Core performance.

—SB

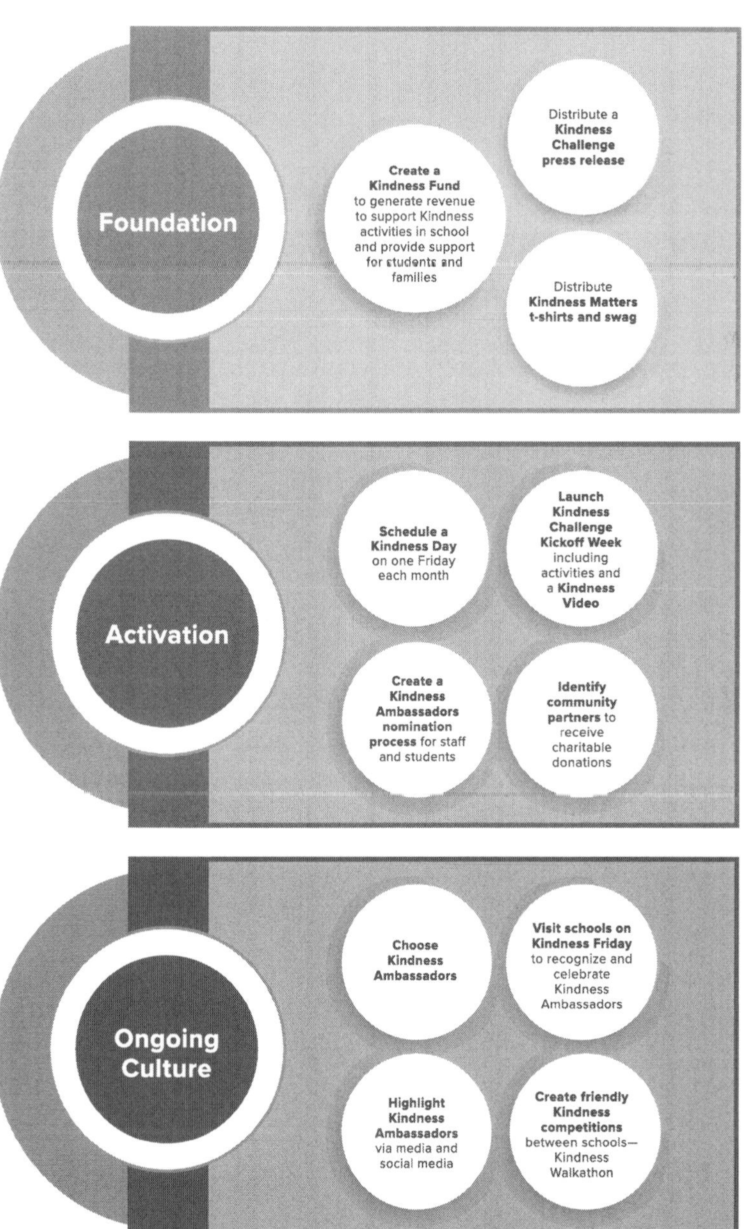
Promoting a Positive School Culture Through Kindness
Foundation
Create a Kindness Fund to generate revenue to support Kindness activities in school and provide support for students and families
Distribute a Kindness Challenge press release
Distribute Kindness Matters t-shirts and swag
Activation
Schedule a Kindness Day on one Friday each month
Launch Kindness Challenge Kickoff Week including activities and a Kindness Video
Create a Kindness Ambassadors nomination process for staff and students
Identify community partners to receive charitable donations
Ongoing Culture
Choose Kindness Ambassadors
Visit schools on Kindness Friday to recognize and celebrate Kindness Ambassadors
Highlight Kindness Ambassadors via media and social media
Create friendly Kindness competitions between schools—Kindness Walkathon

Figure 1

TWO

ABC Student Success Plans

CHAPTER EIGHT

Why Is It the Same Students, Year After Year?

At the start of each school year, we used an activity to remind staff of the powerful influence each of us can potentially have on our students. We asked a simple question: "What factors are inhibiting student success in our school?"

We invited all possible answers and recorded responses in real time. Here were the most common answers:

It's the parents.

The kids don't care.

Students aren't motivated.

I had some of their parents, and they didn't do well in school, either.

We have a lot of students from poverty.

Our number of special education and English as a Second Language students grows every year.

We need more teachers.

We need more instructional assistants.

We don't have enough time for planning.

We have too many meetings.

We need to put more consequences on kids for not completing homework.

We need more slots in the alternative school.

Once we had our initial list generated, we'd ask the next prompt: "Which of these factors can we actually influence?"

Let's place the following in **List A**, a list that says: *We should be able to address these.*

The kids don't care.

Students aren't motivated.

We don't have enough time for planning.

We have too many meetings.

We need to put more consequences on kids for not completing homework.

Let's break these down.

Of these five factors, which have a research base indicating that investing time and effort into them would yield positive outcomes for students?

First, we don't think there's any research that indicates increased consequences for uncompleted homework has a positive impact on student achievement.

Next: we can work with you to address your concerns about having to attend too many meetings and needing increased planning time. In fact, we should be able to work with our leadership team to make those things happen. If those steps help to create a climate of collective teacher efficacy, they're worth going after.

That leaves two items: "The kids don't care." And, "They're not motivated." How do we get them to care and feel connected to school? These are very important observations that we need to address right away.

Now we'll take the remaining factors and create a second list. Let's take a look at **List B.**

It's the parents.

I had some of their parents, and they didn't do well in school, either.

We have a lot of students from poverty.

Our number of special education and English as a Second Language students grows every year.

We need more teachers.

We need more instructional assistants.

We need more slots in the alternative school.

First: how much can we really impact parents' attitude(s) toward school? Can we do anything about the fact that our students' parents didn't do well in school? Certainly, those two things are connected.

Our students can't help it if they have a disability, are living at or under the poverty line, or came here from another country. No one has any control over those things.

Sure, it would be great to add staff and resources. But as we all know, we're in the middle of a recession, and that's not going to happen. We're doing our best to hang onto the staff we have.

The point is: we have *no influence* on the List B factors. Those things may be statistically correlated with student achievement, but they're outside of our locus of control.

In fact, since we can't do anything about them, why don't we just stop talking about them altogether? Doing so is a waste of time and energy. It contributes to a culture of blaming rather than problem-solving.

Our attitude then became: let's get to it! We'll work on less meetings and more planning time for staff. We'll work on getting students more motivated and engaged in school. Who else would like to help us with this work?

As principals, especially ones who had elementary and middle school experience at the time, we were frustrated by the fact that the same students continued to perform poorly in school as they moved across grade levels. Why were the same students who struggled in second grade continuing to struggle in eighth grade?

What were we doing wrong?

How could we take effective action?

Often we want to understand what students are thinking—without directly interacting with them. Sometimes, with exasperation, adults will ask students this question: "What were you thinking?!"

But adults who ask that question rarely wait for the student's answer.

To get to the root of a student problem, *we must talk to students directly and explicitly.* Take the time to do it. It's so important.

Once again, we see the recurring theme of thinking inside the box.

We began to meet individually with students to get to the core of the problem.

Imagine that!

We asked students these questions.

"What do your parents think about your grades? Do they talk to you about them?"

"Do you get in trouble at home when you bring home a report card that looks like this, with all Ds and Fs?"

The answer to the above question was always "No."

What we said next was clear but simple.

"Well, it's not good enough for me or the other adults in this building. And it's not good enough for you. What do you think you could achieve if you tried your hardest?"

The answer to this question was always: "As and Bs."

—SB and GS

CHAPTER NINE

An Idea Is Born (Mad Scientist in a Laboratory)

We began to schedule student meetings during our teachers' planning time, pulling students from specials (phys ed, art, music, etc.) for an initial session. We didn't attempt to schedule parents since we wanted this to be a student-directed plan that led to lasting success.

These students had already informed us that their parents weren't concerned about their grades. Parent/teacher conferences had been held, but improvements in student performance as a result of these conferences were infrequent. Sometimes parents didn't show up for the conferences. At other times, when their children weren't doing well in school, parents naturally felt like they were being blamed, and this led to unpleasant interactions and unsuccessful conferences.

The purpose of a parent/teacher conference for a student who's not doing well in school is to develop a better plan for success moving forward. ABC Student Success Plans addressed that notion.

The first step is for students to choose a trusted adult to meet with on a regular and frequent basis. A lot of times with mentoring programs, the building leaders assume the person students are likely to select as a trusted adult. It's generally because they are superstar teachers with well-deserved reputations for building positive relationships with students.

But there is power in letting students choose. They know who they connect with best. Also, students will often choose someone we don't expect. It could be a teacher from a former grade level, a counselor, physical education teacher, custodian, office staff member, or any number of others. The pool of trusted mentors within a school grows. The chosen adults feel a sense of pride and duty. All these things contribute to a sense of shared purpose.

Students selected their goals in one or more ABC areas: Attendance, Behavior, and Core Performance (grades). Often, these three areas overlap. A student who is not regularly coming to school will definitely struggle to keep up with grades. Students who are failing in school will often misbehave. Students who misbehave miss class time.

These are tough cycles to break. But it can be done.

Students stated what they would do, and the teacher or staff listed, for support, the commitments they would make. For example, a student who is struggling in a class has the problem that they don't have parental approval to stay for tutoring to get their grades up. The holdup? No permission slip from the parent. The school contacts the parent and facilitates their approval. Now the student can stay after school to receive individualized or small group instruction from the teacher.

A few outcomes are likely to occur.

- The teacher appreciates the extra effort the student is demonstrating.
- The student improves their grade in that class.
- The teacher/student relationship is strengthened.

ABC Student Success Plans were born. Those plans looked like this:

In the following chapter, we share five highly successful student success plan examples.

Trust us, it was hard to narrow it down to five.

—SB and GS

Student Success Plan

NAME:

A — ATTENDANCE

Goal(s): Initiative and Self Direction

STUDENT ACTION STEPS: Social Responsibility	ADMINISTRATOR/STAFF ACTION STEPS: Problem Solving
Choose an item.	Choose an item.

B — BEHAVIOR

Goal(s): Initiative and Self Direction

STUDENT ACTION STEPS: Social Responsibility	ADMINISTRATOR/STAFF ACTION STEPS: Problem Solving
Choose an item.	Choose an item.

C — CORE PERFORMANCE

Goal(s): Initiative and Self Direction

STUDENT ACTION STEPS: Social Responsibility	ADMINISTRATOR/STAFF ACTION STEPS: Problem Solving
Choose an item.	Choose an item.

Figure 2

CHAPTER TEN

ABC Success Stories

An Attendance Story

One elementary school I was supervising had a fifth-grade girl who was struggling socially and emotionally in school. She began to refuse to ride the bus because she didn't want to come to school anymore. So her mother began to drive her to school in the mornings, and every day was a power struggle. Inevitably, once she got to her classroom, the student would claim she was sick and ask to go to the clinic. The nurse would call the mother, the child would get picked up early, and the cycle of truancy would continue.

After speaking with the principal about the power of ABC Student Success Plans, the student decided to give it a try. Of the three areas, improving performance for students who are struggling with attendance is often the most difficult. But we had experienced something important: when students are given meaningful school jobs, they're more motivated to attend.

The principal asked the student: "What job would you really be interested in here at school?"

The student replied: "School safety patrol."

The principal told her that it's imperative for safety patrols to arrive at school early. If the student could begin to ride the bus every day, she was told, she could be a school safety patrol member. The student was elated and said she would hold up her end of the deal. It was formalized in writing using an ABC Student Success Plan.

While all this was happening, I warned the principal that there might be a backlash from other students, parents, or staff. I explained that they might not feel this student deserved to be a safety patrol, that she had not "earned it" like other students.

We discussed a proper response, and we understood that we need to differentiate with students all the time, with academics and in other areas. In order to move students forward and help them own their learning, we need to meet them where they are.

The student held up her end of the deal.

The principal's actions built trust with both the student and her parent. It was obvious to both that the principal was sincerely trying to help by being solution-oriented. The principal had made an important connection and learned a lesson that could be replicated as often as needed with other students.

For her part, the student now had a group of peers to identify with. She was an important person in her school: a safety patrol member! She enjoyed the chance to finally have a friend group. According to the principal, the student's favorite part of her new role was helping younger students each day. She came to understand that the younger students needed her every day and looked forward to interacting with her. In essence, this student was paying it forward.

—Garett Smith

A Behavior Story

After moving on from the principalship, I was able to help administrators in a larger school division implement ABC Student Success Plans (SSPs) across all levels: elementary, middle, and high school. We would meet at regular intervals to discuss student progress.

I was working with a particularly creative elementary school assistant principal who had a third-grade boy who was experiencing a very specific behavioral problem: whenever his behavior was corrected by his teacher, he felt compelled to talk back.

He just had to have the last word. I'm not sure if there's any behavior that annoys teachers more.

After weeks of effort, the clever assistant principal decided to try a new tack. She provided the student with his own special journal. Whenever he was overcome with a desire to talk back, the plan read, he would instead write his comment in his journal. The idea was working very well.

All teachers who worked with this student were provided a copy of his student success plan. As soon as he indicated a compulsion to talk back in class, they would simply redirect him: "Remember your comment journal!"

I asked the assistant principal if I could meet the student. When we met, I asked him: "Can I see your journal?" The student shook his head no. The assistant principal pointed out that that was part of the agreement written into the plan. For the student to comply with the process, the teacher needed to maintain the dignity of his privacy. I said that I understood.

The journal was to be destroyed on the last day of school, but up until that time it was a useful tool for a struggling student that simultaneously benefited his teacher, his classmates, and himself.

I learned later from the assistant principal that the student didn't need to use the comment journal when he returned to school the following year. Ultimately, the behavior itself had been extinguished! Scaffolding, in the form of a comment journal, was no longer needed.

—Garett Smith

A Core Performance Story

Jazmine came from a large and well-known family in the community, many of whom had not traditionally experienced academic success in school. When it came time for a team of her teachers, counselor, and principal to meet with Jazmine to develop an ABC SSP during her eighth-grade year, it was obvious to everyone that she needed a goal in the area of Core Performance.

There were no issues with her behavior or attendance. To her credit, Jazmine chose a goal of making A/B Honor Roll for the first time in her life. All of her teachers knew Jazmine's goal and were rooting for her to succeed despite seemingly long odds.

Weeks later, our school had an Honor Roll breakfast for all qualifying students.

Jazmine was there.

I said: "Jazmine, I'm so proud of you for making the Honor Roll! What is the key to your success so I can tell other students who are also trying to achieve this accomplishment for the first time?"

Jazmine looked at me and said: "Don't you remember, Dr. Smith? It was when we had that meeting and I set the goal for myself!"

The core theory behind student success plans is twofold: first, students need to own their learning, and goal-setting is one example. Second, students are more likely to experience success in school and not give up when paired with a trusted adult.

Unlike earlier, less effective behavior plans or attendance contracts, the terms aren't being dictated to the student by an adult.

Rather, it's an agreement by both parties to help the student achieve a goal they've selected for themselves.

Students own their learning when they:

- Know their current level of understanding
- Understand where they're going and have the confidence to take on the challenge
- Select tools to guide their learning
- Seek feedback and recognize errors are opportunities to learn
- Monitor progress and adjust their learning
- Recognize their learning and teach others

—Garett Smith

A Worker Bee

I've met a lot of students over the years, but few have the sheer talent for classroom disruption that Daniel possessed. He was the kind of kid who annoyed everyone, including himself, it seemed.

The reports came in weekly: talking out of turn, tapping on the desk, wandering the room, arguing with peers over who had the better sneakers—the list went on and on. His teachers were at their wit's end, labeling him everything from "distractible" to "defiant." They were focused on the outcome (disruption), but missed the input (energy).

When Daniel landed in my office for the third time in a month, I knew the standard consequence wasn't going to work. He didn't want to sit in in-school suspension. Frankly, he didn't want to sit anywhere associated with school.

I took the time to implement an ABC Student Success Plan. The point of it is: it goes beyond a list of rules. We focused on the root cause of his behavior, or as we call it, "the awareness of the trigger." What I learned about Daniel changed everything.

He wasn't a malicious kid. He was a worker bee.

In the field of education, you learn that some people are just built to move. They need to be doing, building, or fixing something. That was Daniel. He just needed to be out working.

The breakthrough moment came when he quietly admitted the truth: "I just don't like being home alone." His energy in school was a direct symptom of his loneliness and lack of productive engagement outside of it.

That realization shifted our focus from punishment to purpose.

I put our ABC Success Plan into action, but instead of focusing on, or demanding, classroom silence, we focused on channeling his energy.

I started utilizing him.

Daniel became my shadow, my most reliable employee. He helped me with everything: picking up the mountain of trash left after a Friday night dance, moving boxes, reorganizing the athletic supply closet. He even helped me build a simple bookshelf for my office (which, by the way, is still standing). He'd show up after school buzzing with energy and ready to just *work*.

He was focused, productive, and happy. When he was working, all the previous negative labels—the talker, the wanderer, the arguer—disappeared. He had found his purpose.

Our relationship, built on equity and mutual respect, taught him that his energy wasn't a deficit; it was a gift. That's the real lesson in the ABC Success Plans; they are about fixing the kid's environment, not just fixing the kid.

When Daniel finished the eighth grade, he was still prone to tapping his pen, but he was also a leader and a trusted hand. On his last day, I looked him in the eye and made him a promise.

"Daniel," I said, "you are a worker. Don't ever stop moving. I promise you a job, no matter where I am working. You call me when you need one."

That promise still stands.

Daniel's "defiance" was really just misdirected industriousness. The Student Success Plan must be flexible enough to identify the underlying need behind the misbehavior.

- **The action:** Leaders must look past the paperwork and ask: *what is this child trying to achieve with this behavior?* When a student constantly seeks movement, give them a meaningful task that requires movement (delivery, organization, mentoring). This shifts the focus from managing a student's lack of attention to leveraging that abundant energy. The ABC Plan here transitioned from an accountability tool to an asset-based deployment strategy.

Remember: kindness matters. This is the promise of purpose.

The ultimate act of kindness for a worker bee is giving them work. It validates their existence and shows you believe in their utility.

- **The action:** Look for non-traditional ways to engage high-energy students. Put them on a custodial or facilities team, make them the principal's runner, or assign them to organize community service drives. When you give a kid a genuine, important task, you teach them responsibility and self-worth. It says, "I trust you with this." And that is far more powerful than saying, "I trust you to be quiet."

Remember continuous improvement: it yields a lifetime commitment.

The relationship-building extends far beyond the school year. When leaders make promises and keep them, it builds a legacy of trust in the institution and in the adults.

- **The action:** The promise I made to Daniel wasn't just a friendly goodbye; it was the capstone on his Student Success Plan. It reinforced the core belief that his effort and his nature were valuable in the real world. This type of personal investment is the true engine of continuous school improvement, as it creates students who are ready and willing to contribute positively to society.

A Message to Daniel:

Daniel, if you happen to read this book and need a job, call me. Seriously. I got you.

—Stenette Byrd

Cut from a Different Cloth

It was the first day of school and I was the new principal. Lunchtime had finally come. I saw a student walking through the cafeteria with the swagger of a king who owned the place. Eventually he cut into line, completing ignoring those who had been waiting patiently. I walked over to the young man (whom I would come to find out is Clarence), as any responsible principal would do, and politely asked him to move to the back of the line. He turned, and the look in his eyes wasn't just defiance; it was pure fire. He delivered the kind of line that makes time stop in a high school cafeteria: "Who the 'f' are you?" That was followed by: "You better get the 'f' out of my face. You don't know me. I'm cut from a different cloth."

The blood rushed to my face. Every disciplinary reflex honed over years of leadership screamed at me to react. But a different voice, one built on the foresight of relationship-first leadership, whispered: *Wait.*

* * *

Three weeks earlier, I was excited to be the new principal of King's Fork High School. Knowing the importance of building student connections, I spent those weeks before the first day of school attending all fall sports practices and meeting with coaches and students. I introduced myself and listened to their ideas about how to make "their" school a safe and welcoming place. Before the first day of school, I had gotten to know hundreds of students, teachers, and coaches. I was ready for anything that would come my way.

* * *

Now fast-forward back to that cafeteria and Clarence. There I was, standing face to face with this young man . . . before I could open my mouth to say the first thing, dozens of students walked over, grabbed Clarence, and said to him: "Clarence, chill. He's cool. He's our new principal. Now stop cutting people and go to the back of the line."

Clarence was stunned. His face went from aggressive fire to confused shock. The peer pressure, fueled by my previously established connections, instantly dissolved the conflict. He slowly, sheepishly, walked to the back of the line.

Clarence's aggressive outburst was a desperate move to save face and project toughness. Punishing him publicly, after he'd already been corrected by his peers, would have guaranteed resentment and a future battle. This is where *strategic kindness does indeed matter.*

- **The action:** I waited until lunch was over and called Clarence to my office. We didn't talk about the line-cutting. We talked about his frustration, his "trigger." I asked him: "What made you feel like you had to explode like that? Let's find out what made you feel like you had to act that way." We focused on his behavior in a private, supportive space, allowing him to save face.

Student Success Plans: The ABC Blueprint

During that private conversation, we discussed the underlying issue and created a forward-looking ABC Success Plan.

- **The action:** The ABC Success Plan was simple (and here we used the ABC in a little different way): **A**wareness of the Trigger (feeling disrespected or ignored); **B**reak the Cycle (take three deep breaths before replying to an adult); and **C**ommunicate the Need (instead of swearing, use respectful language to express frustration). By giving Clarence a tangible plan, we empowered him to be the author of his own success. The goal wasn't just compliance, it was helping him manage the emotions that prevented him from reaching his goals.

Continuous Improvement: Consistency and Compassion

Over the next few weeks I made a point to check in with Clarence daily. A simple nod or a quick "How's the ABC plan going?" in the hallway. Our relationship developed naturally. He was still "cut from a different cloth," but now that cloth was actually communicating respect, not rebellion.

I wish I could report that Clarence became one of the school's most passionate, protective student advocates, but I can report that he never returned to the principal's office again.

—Stenette Byrd

CHAPTER ELEVEN

Scaling Up ABC Student Success Plans

In 2012 I had the opportunity to go back to Newport News Public Schools (NNPS) where I started my career as a teacher. The opportunity included supervising and developing school leaders at the elementary school level.

Like many school divisions, particularly urban ones, student behavior was a primary focus of conversation among staff. The various schools had their own systems in place. Some went school-wide with tiered systems of support; others simply cherry-picked parts of that program. There was not a universal model in place to help students who were struggling with attendance, behavior, or academics.

Of course, many students were identified as needing support through the child study process, through the formation of an individualized education plan, or a 504 plan; these were needed to address struggles in any of the three aforementioned areas. We had very smart school leaders working together to track and analyze student data from schools. There were disparities in all three areas based on race, disability, and socioeconomic status.

These are the stubborn school problems mentioned in the title of this book. What we were doing at the time wasn't working. We knew it wasn't working because we didn't see positive results in our data. It's important to understand that there's no way of knowing if your approach to these problems is working *until* it shows up in your data.

During one of the meetings with NNPS leaders, I was able to share our ideas about individualized student success plans from my days as a principal. They weren't IEPs, and they weren't 504 plans. They weren't behavior contracts. We weren't attempting to set up a token economy to encourage students to act in positive ways.

Rather, they were simply contracts between a student who was struggling in school and a trusted adult of their choice. We were taking our approach down to the most granular, individualized level for students. Our group of leaders, understanding the power of relationships in school, agreed to give the model a try.

We wanted to make sure we could implement this model across all three levels: elementary, middle, and high school. The first thing needed was to schedule a kickoff event to introduce the concept to all of our leaders working throughout the school division. We set up an initial training on a warm summer morning in a cafeteria of an old building that no longer served students. I'm pretty sure the air conditioning wasn't working.

A smaller group of us had broken off to plan the session. We knew that administrators could sometimes be skeptical when a new program was being introduced, especially if they've never heard of it before and don't have any confidence that it will be helpful to them, their staff, and their students.

So we decided we needed to thump the audience in the heart right from the outset of the presentation.

One of our high school assistant principals, Diron Ford, shared a compelling story about a student named Jahad. He had invited Jahad to attend our session that morning. At this time Jahad was attending a small college and playing basketball. Jahad came in that morning, dressed in a suit, but looking nervous to speak to a group of school administrators.

Who wouldn't be? His mother accompanied him.

Jahad carried a sheaf of handwritten notes in his hand as he stepped to the lectern. He cleared his throat. Then he began to tell us about his experiences as a middle and high school student. He was certain, he said, that teachers and administrators didn't like him, and he got suspended frequently. When he matriculated to his high school, our assistant principal, Mr. Ford, who had read something of his history in middle school, reached out to form a relationship with him.

However, Jahad's circle of trust was very small, and it certainly didn't include any school administrators!

As Jahad explained to the group that morning, he continued to make bad choices in school and associate with others who were doing the same. Finally, Assistant Principal Ford had no choice but to send Jahad to alternative school for a semester.

Then, according to Jahad, the strangest thing happened. Assistant Principal Ford continued to reach out to him, even making in-person visits to the alternative school. Jahad wondered aloud to the audience, saying exactly what he was thinking at the time: "Why isn't this guy giving up on me?" Jahad decided he needed to give this man a chance.

When he returned from alternative school, he started checking in regularly with Assistant Principal Ford, and they formed a productive and meaningful relationship. Jahad described how he improved his grades and was more discreet about who he associated with. He was now a college student-athlete!

The audience gave him a rousing ovation.

Then something unexpected happened.

Unplanned, Jahad's mother stood and came to the lectern. Like the rest of us, she was deeply touched by Jahad's words. Through her tears, she pleaded with the group.

"Please, please, please. I know you are all school administrators, and you have a tremendous influence on young people's lives.

"But please hear my message. Don't ever give up on a student like Jahad because you see what's possible when somebody believes in a young person!"

A standing ovation ensued. We were hoping for one thump on the heart, but we got two! Mission accomplished!

Our building leaders were ready to give this new model a chance. We moved on to hosting professional development sessions at the individual schools for administrators and counselors. Soon we had things up and running.

Our superintendent wanted to see the program in action, so once a month we would visit schools to meet with students and hear their stories. It became my favorite day of the month. We listened to students share about how helpless they felt when they came back to class after getting kicked out because they didn't understand anything upon their return . . . so they just gave up. Or that they were the kid who never got invited to a friend's house to play because they were always in trouble in school. It was heartbreaking—and yet beautiful—at the same time.

It was beautiful because they were stories of success: "This is how things used to go for me in school, but this is how they go for me now!"

One of my favorite questions to ask in these interviews was this: "Do you notice that adults are treating you differently now, both in school and at home?" The "aha moments" were priceless.

We often say this, and it's true: "no kid wants to suck in school." Every student wants to be successful in school, to be accepted by the peers and adults in their lives.

Once Dr. Byrd and I tried to use "No Kid Wants to Suck in School" as the name for a presentation we were invited to give, but we received pushback from Old Dominion University when we submitted it. So we modified the title to more accurately state the purpose of the ABC SSPs.

"The Power of ABC Student Success Plans: A Tool to Help Struggling Students Help Themselves."

Notice the transfer of responsibility.

—Garett Smith

CHAPTER TWELVE

The Practitioner's Script

The "Script" is a structured series of questions designed to serve as a tool for school administrators, counselors, and teachers when following up with students participating in an ABC Student Success Plan. This tool encourages meaningful dialogue that helps students assess their own progress, identify growth areas, and recognize the positive changes they have achieved.

The Script is about a meaningful conversation. It's the beginning of a framework that builds student ownership of learning. When students can articulate their journey, describe the strategies that have worked, and share insights with their peers, they move from being passive recipients of support to active agents in their own success. In fact, one of the clearest indicators that a student truly understands a concept or strategy is their ability to teach it to others. This peer-to-peer exchange strengthens confidence, deepens learning, and contributes to a culture of mutual support across the school community.

The Purpose of the Plan

It's important to remember that a Student Success Plan is not meant to be permanent. The ultimate goal of any intervention or support plan is to help the student develop the skills, habits, and self-awareness necessary to eventually manage their learning and growth independently. As educators, we must continuously communicate this message:

> *Being on a plan is not a punishment or a life sentence. It's a temporary support designed to help students build the tools they need to succeed on their own.*
>
> —Garett Smith

In educational terms, this process is known as scaffolding. Scaffolding provides structured support at the beginning of the learning journey and gradually removes that support as the student becomes more capable and confident. Just as scaffolding is removed from a building once it can stand on its own, the same applies to students: once they begin experiencing consistent success, the scaffolding can be removed.

Using the Script to Provide Closure

The Script can serve as a meaningful bridge between structured support and independence. It allows administrators and mentors to guide students through a reflective process that celebrates growth and identifies next steps. This process also provides emotional closure. It helps students recognize that they've achieved a milestone and are ready for new challenges.

Sample reflective questions are included in this chart.

Partners for Student Success

NAME: ______________________________

GUIDING QUESTION	NOTES
Can you tell us about your Student Success Plan?	
What was happening before you started with your Student Success Plan?	
Which adults are currently helping you at school? Have you noticed that adults are treating you differently at home and at school since you started having more success?	
How do you think that there is a connection between your attendance, behavior, and grades?	
What advice would you give to another student who was struggling in school?	
How would you help another student who was struggling?	

Figure 3

Through these conversations, educators can reinforce resilience, agency, and accountability. Students begin to internalize that success is not a destination, but a *process* they have learned to navigate.

The Role of Trusted Adults

The impact of the Script and the success of the Student Success Plan depends heavily on the presence of trusted adult relationships. Students thrive when they feel seen, heard, and supported by adults who believe in them. This relationship builds the foundation for honest reflection and sustained motivation.

Educators who interact with students over multiple years often have a unique advantage in this process. These trusted figures may include administrators, school counselors, fine arts teachers, physical education teachers, and coaches. Their long-term relationships allow for continuity, deeper understanding of the student's personal growth, and consistent reinforcement of positive behaviors.

When these adults use the Script effectively, they not only help students reflect on past progress, they also set the stage for future success. The combination of reflection, relationship, and responsibility transforms the experience from a school intervention into a life lesson in perseverance and self-efficacy.

Please don't forget that the trusted adult can be *anyone*. It does not have to be the child's teacher or even a teacher at all. When selecting this adult, ask the student for input: "Who can you go to in this school if you need help?"

Don't Mess This Part Up

The success of any Student Success Plan depends largely on the quality of the relationship between the student and the adult guiding the process. Tools like the Script are only as effective as the trust that exists between the two people using them. When a strong connection is present, reflection feels authentic, progress feels achievable, and the student begins to take ownership of their learning. But when the wrong adult is paired with a student, even the best-designed plan can lose its power. In some cases, it can unintentionally reinforce the very barriers the plan was meant to remove.

Every student responds differently to authority, communication styles, and personalities. Some thrive under gentle encouragement while others respond best to clear, direct structure. When an adult's approach doesn't align with the student's needs, the result can be disengagement, frustration, or avoidance. A mismatch might look like a student who shuts down during meetings, offers minimal responses, or avoids contact altogether. The adult may perceive this as defiance; in reality, it is often a form of self-protection.

Without genuine rapport, students are unlikely to open up, reflect meaningfully, or internalize new strategies.
—Stenette Byrd

Trust lies at the heart of this process. The Script requires honesty and vulnerability, qualities that only emerge when a student feels safe and respected. If the adult leading the conversation has not yet earned that trust, or if there is a history of misunderstanding between them, reflection quickly becomes superficial. The student may say what they think the adult wants to hear just to get through the meeting. When this happens, the process becomes transactional rather than transformational.

There are usually warning signs when the adult-student pairing isn't working. The student might resist meeting times, appear disengaged during conversations, or show little improvement in attendance, behavior, or academics. These signs should not be ignored or seen as personal failures. Instead, they should be treated as feedback that the current support structure needs adjusting. In such cases, schools should act quickly to make a change. Reassigning a student to another trusted adult can make a world of difference—especially when the new mentor already has a positive connection with the student.

When making this kind of change, it's important to communicate the purpose clearly and positively. Students should understand that switching mentors isn't a setback; it's an intentional step to ensure they get the best possible support. Likewise, staff should view the reassignment process as an opportunity to learn and reflect on how mentors are selected and trained. It can be helpful to hold a brief transition conversation between the outgoing and incoming adults so information is shared, progress is preserved, and the student doesn't feel as though they're starting over.

Intentional pairing is essential from the start. Schools should avoid random assignments and instead consider each student's individual needs, personality, and existing relationships. Factors such as shared interests, communication style, and consistency of interaction should guide these decisions. This is especially important for students who have experienced trauma, instability, or repeated negative interactions with adults. For those students, one genuine connection can change the entire trajectory of their school experience.

When the right adult is chosen, the Script becomes more than a tool—it becomes a bridge to confidence, growth, and independence. *When the wrong adult is chosen*, that same process can feel hollow. The difference lies not in the plan itself, but in the relationship that supports it.

A Final Note

For any school initiative to be successful, one staff member needs to be designated to oversee it and serve as its champion. Of course, this is difficult because everyone already has a full plate.

Still, the power of ABC success plans is so potentially impactful on unsuccessful students that it's worth seeking the best way to implement. Perhaps responsibilities can be shifted to free up time for the champion of this initiative. Providing a stipend is another possible solution.

As you'll read about in our conclusion section, if it's worth doing, there's always a way!

* * *

By the end of the second section of this book, *ABC Student Success Plans,* we have moved from ideas to action. We've discussed building systems that give every student a chance to succeed through focused attention on attendance, behavior, and core performance. Those stories have been about turning compassion into structure and giving our good intentions a successful framework.

However, as any educator knows, the work of improvement never truly ends. Once the systems are in place, a new realization emerges: sustaining success. This requires more than just a plan, it demands continuous reflection, collaboration, and growth among the adults who make the work happen every day. *Section Three: A Cycle of Continuous School Improvement* explores that next phase of the journey. We shift the focus from student-level plans to schoolwide practices: those deliberate observations, conversations, and actions that keep a school moving forward one improvement cycle at a time.

—SB and GS

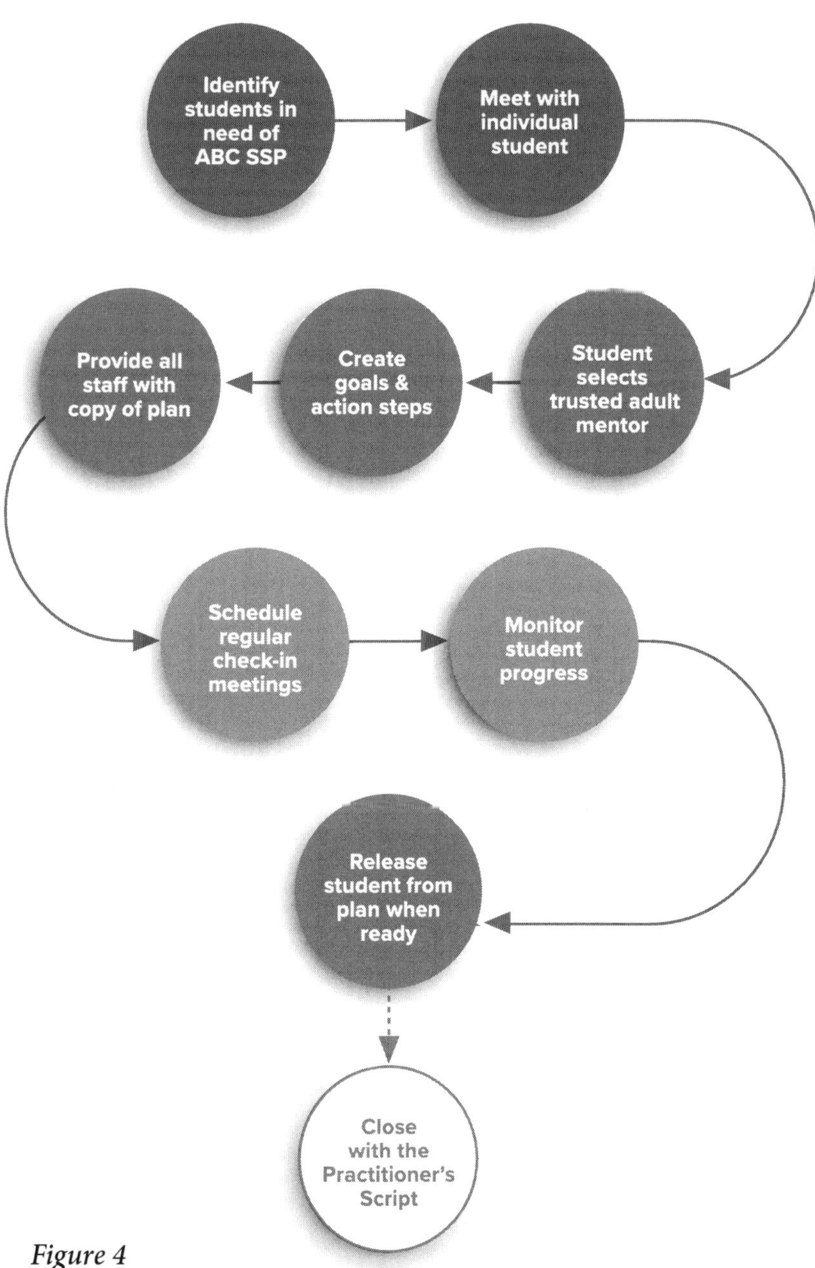
ABC Student Success Plan Process
Identify students in need of ABC SSP
Meet with individual student
Student selects trusted adult mentor
Create goals & action steps
Provide all staff with copy of plan
Schedule regular check-in meetings
Monitor student progress
Release student from plan when ready
Close with the Practitioner's Script

Figure 4

THREE

A Cycle of Continuous School Improvement

CHAPTER THIRTEEN

Practices That Move the Needle

As we worked through our school leadership careers in the era of high-stakes testing and accountability, several proposed solutions emerged as schools and school divisions under pressure searched for the keys to success. Over the years we recall the focus shifting constantly.

"We need to focus more on vocabulary!" More of this thinking was: we've stopped teaching vocabulary, and that's why our students aren't performing well on the tests!

"We need zero tolerance policies for students who commit discipline infractions!" More: this small percentage of students is preventing other students from learning and keeping our teachers from teaching.

"We need more technology!" Learners are different today, and our traditional way of teaching is too slow and unengaging for them.

"We need to build stamina!" The tests are too long for our students, so we need to train their brains to focus longer, much like building physical stamina through regular exercising.

"Our students don't understand the language on the test!" We need to teach them what the questions are asking. Let's try plain English SOL tests.

As it turned out, none of the proposed solutions, in isolation, was the answer.

That's because there is no silver bullet solution to school improvement.

It requires a continuum of focused practices and interventions. Not only is there no one-stop solution to school improvement, there are also no shortcuts for school leaders. They must do the work. It all starts with a smart plan that's easy to communicate and engenders buy-in from staff.

Let's focus on the research. We all know which educational practices work best.

We all took the same classes.

Since public schools have limited resources, it's important to focus our efforts on the instructional practices that yield the highest impacts. According to John Hattie's meta-analysis:

What Works

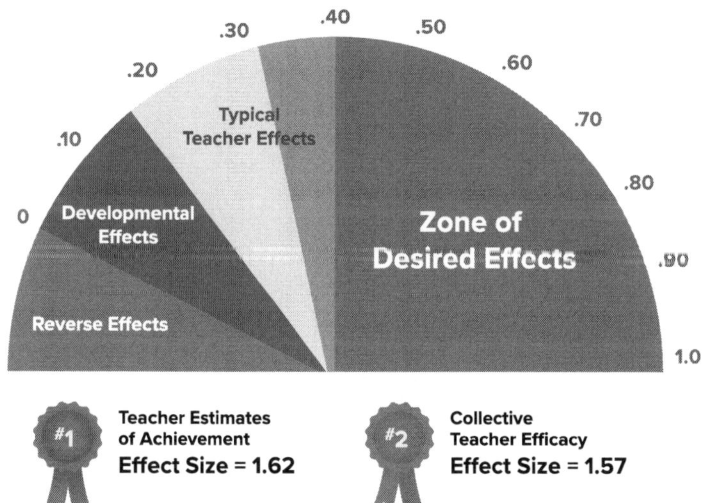

"Our job is to help kids ***exceed what they think they can do*** *... which means giving them the confidence that they can do it and teaching them the skills so that they can do it."*

— HATTIE, SELF-REPORTED GRADES (VIDEO FILE), MAY 2, 2012.
https://vimeo.com/41465488

"Collective teacher efficacy is not just rah-rah thinking ... It's the combined belief that ***it is US that causes learning.*** *When you believe that you can make the difference, and then you feed it with the evidence that you are, that is dramatically powerful."*

— HATTIE, COLLECTIVE EFFICACY (VIDEO FILE), MAY 1, 2018.
https://vimeo.com/267382804

"The Visible Learning model isn't one in which the leader is a hero who does everything alone. Improving outcomes ***requires a team*** *of teachers, students, parents, and community members, all working in collaboration.* ***The team works together to agree on the nature of success throughout the year.****"*

Figure 5

Teacher estimates of student achievement simply means that teachers believe in the ability of their students to learn. Collective teacher efficacy means teachers believe in their own abilities as a team to teach students effectively. One reflects teachers' high expectations for students; the other reflects the educators' high expectations for themselves.

It's not fluff. It's right there in the research.

Remember, a 0.4 effect size represents one year of learning across one calendar school year. Anything above 1.0 is a powerful instructional practice. These two variables provide two of the highest effect sizes.

Focus on the research and put it into practice.

Along the way, if you want to progress on a path of continuous improvement, it's critical that all staff gain instructional expertise. All the adults need to be speaking the same language so there is consistency in expectations across classrooms for students.

Here is a simple philosophy or guidepost for leading people. It doesn't matter if you're a parent, coach, teacher, principal, or superintendent. These three simple points work.

These elements have to be in place and in order. The third element is especially important. You want to provide support through conversations, modeling, and active listening. However, if you provide too much support, the individual or team won't grow.

The intention is to *build capacity.* Again, it's important to transfer the responsibility for learning to the learner, regardless of whether that learner is a student or an adult.

The biggest change that occurs when an educator matriculates from the classroom to a coaching or leadership position

Figure 6

is simply this: as a teacher, you are charged with teaching students. As a coach or administrator, you are also responsible for teaching adults.

A useful metaphor for building capacity in others is learning to ride a bicycle. Someone helped you ride a bike as much as they possibly could. Maybe it was one of your parents or an older sibling.

At some point, though, that person had to let go of that seat and turn you loose.

Learning to swim is another example. The instructor can give you encouragement, tips, and demonstrations, but the task is only accomplished when the learner is able to swim on his or her own.

For school improvement to be sustainable and continuous, it takes everyone. The effective school improvement leader understands this and focuses on building capacity in others.

Make the team you have better.

—SB and GS

CHAPTER FOURTEEN

The Power of Classroom Presence

I still remember my first ever formal meeting as a new superintendent with principals, assistant principals, and central office staff. I wanted to make sure these leaders in our schools understood there are no shortcuts or silver bullets for school improvement.

You have to do the work, and there has to be urgency around it. As I sensed my message wasn't reaching a couple of them, I changed tack and delivered an intentionally jarring statement.

"If you're not spending your time in classrooms, I don't know what the hell you're working on!"

I could tell by their reaction that I now had everyone's attention.

The reality for school leaders is that if you aren't in classrooms every day, you truly don't know what's happening in your school. You might think you do. But you don't.

I've heard all the excuses about time constraints, student discipline, unexpected visitors dropping in, and more. I'm not buying any of them.

When your focus is on classroom instruction, everything else will come together.

Time constraints won't be an issue because your daily and weekly schedules will be built around classroom visits and observations.

You'll deal with fewer student discipline issues because students will see you all the time. I promise that if you wait in your office, student discipline will come to you.

What message are you sending students by being in classrooms? What message are you sending when you aren't?

Unexpected visitors cannot be allowed to disrupt your instructional practices. You're in charge. Ensure that your office staff knows that classroom observation time is sacred time and cannot be interrupted—unless it's an absolute emergency.

Word will spread quickly among families that it's imperative to make an appointment to meet—just like with every other profession!

How do you work with all school staff to build an organizational culture where high expectations for academic achievement are the most important focus?

Can your staff answer these questions?

- For teachers: how do students know that their academic performance in your classroom is the most important thing to you?
- For principals: how do students know that their academic performance in your school is the most important thing to you?

This is a great question to ask these groups at the beginning of the year, midyear, and toward the end of the year. Save their responses to share throughout the year.

This will give the entire faculty a toolbox of tangible actions to implement and help convey to students what's most important.

A parallel exists between what great teachers do in their classrooms and what great principals do in their schools. Both have high expectations for self. Both seek continuous professional improvement and development and understand this maxim:

When adults get smarter, so do our students.

Educational equity is achieved when we have great teaching taking place in every classroom.

The holy grail in schools is achieved when all of your student groups are performing at a high level regardless of race, ethnicity, economic status, or disability. This is achieved through a laser focus on classroom instruction and learning. You won't know if what you're doing is working until it shows up in your data.

In addition to closing gaps with academic achievement, schools need to work intelligently to close gaps between subgroups in our two other measures of school success: student discipline and attendance. This is why ABC Student Success Plans, described in the second section of this book, focus on these three critical areas.

The overall plan has to be coherent and work together in the same direction for continuous improvement.

—GS

CHAPTER FIFTEEN

Beyond the Checklist: Meaningful Classroom Observations and Tools

Now that you know your master plan includes frequent classroom observations and feedback, it's time to share expectations with teachers and staff. They need to know exactly what you're looking for.

Just like when communicating to students, be explicit. Confused teachers are stressed-out teachers. It's imperative that they understand the "why" and the end goal. The end goal, simply, is to have great teaching taking place in every classroom.

For every lesson, we'll be looking for a learning target, success criteria, and some type of formative assessment. Practice together. Let teachers use the tools in staff meetings to evaluate through a short classroom teaching video. There are many things like this you can do.

Share common expectations to establish a baseline for what effective instruction looks like. Here are a few simple examples.

- If we don't see your learning target or hear it stated, expect that we'll ask you about it.
- If there is more than one adult in the classroom during the observation, we expect both to be working with individual or small groups of students. Why? Because it's the fastest and most effective way to move students academically.
- You should expect that observers will sit with students to ask what they're working on and why. The reason? Students need to know what they're learning and be able to explain why it's important. It sets a purpose and answers the age-old student question: why do we need to learn this anyway? (Plus, it's fun!)

This graphic provides a visual for shared expectations among the entire faculty.

Use these lesson observations to look for key assessments.

At first, teachers will be uncomfortable with this practice. That's why it's important to establish norms for evaluators in this model. It's designed to be a collaborative approach to student achievement. Here are guidelines to making key observations.

We know that classroom instruction will improve through formal observations and meaningful feedback. In essence, as a school leader, you're constantly repeating your message through your actions. Great instruction is the most important

Lesson Observations

1 Learning Intentions and Success Criteria

- What standard(s) are being addressed?
- How does this align with curriculum framework?
- How do students have understanding of what and why they are learning?
- Is there evidence of learning intentions & success criteria posted and/or visible for students?

2 Learning Activities

- What are the activities during this time?
- Do activities align with the framework and learning intentions/success criteria?
- What are students doing during this time?
- Are the activities engaging/high-yield strategies?

3 Formative Assessment

- What formative or other assessment is being used?
- How does the teacher know that students understand?
- For example, is there evidence of the teacher noting student's performance on a task to be used for future planning/grouping, etc.?
- Does the assessment align with the learning intentions/success criteria? Are students able to use the assessment to determine if they have understanding?

Figure 7

Observation Guidelines

The purpose of observations is to accelerate learning for our students and build relationships among staff. Staff must trust us in order to be open to suggestions. Remember, learning is a partnership, and we are support.

- Always approach classrooms with a positive greeting, which may include:
  - Speaking/Smiling to the classroom teacher upon entering
  - Talking with students about their learning
  - Thanking the classroom teacher upon exiting for letting us visit
- Avoid interrupting instruction or the flow of instruction.
- Aim for 5 observations per week; we encourage schools to design a schedule to help know who is going to which location.
- The school division will also be maintaining an observation list by employees — Our goal is that by the end of the first semester, 100% of employees have received feedback.
- Provide written feedback as quickly as possible, but no later than a week after the visit. School Leadership tip with paperwork: Touch it once!
- Have a follow-up conversation with the teacher OR notify the teacher of the observation through an email.
- Staff may use the form-sharing as an option. Make sure all forms are finalized in TalentEd within a week.

thing to all of us, regardless of our position in this teaching and learning organization. It takes everyone.

What else happens when school leaders are frequently in classrooms?

Doing so facilitates relationship-building with staff and students. You've shared common experiences. You may even have participated in learning activities alongside the students. You've got material to work with!

Now it doesn't seem odd if you ask a teacher how that lesson turned out: "I'm sorry that I couldn't stay all the way to the end, but I'm dying to know how students performed on that formative assessment."

Talking to students about their grades is perfectly natural: "Wow, you were on fire in Ms. Jones's class the other day. Do you currently have an A in her class?"

You learn people's names much more quickly. Please don't discount the importance of that factor. It's basic respect. You can't possibly preach about respect if you don't model it for your students and staff.

CHAPTER SIXTEEN

The Cycle

Every school and school division needs a master plan for instruction. It needs to be rooted in sound research, and it needs to be simple and easy to communicate and understand. Once it's in place and teachers start experiencing quick wins in their student achievement data, buy-in will follow.

In Staunton City Schools, we use the model shown below to convey what we believe is the most important instructional work: we call it our System of Support. We believe it's the work in the classroom that matters most. In order to truly impact student achievement, a great deal of time is spent here.

It starts with observations and feedback. All of our school administrators are expected to complete at least five observations per week, and we support them in this process. We have weekly check-ins at each of our schools (school principal with the superintendent, Student Services, and Instruction), and we often use this time to get into classrooms.

In addition, we schedule days for observations in the schools each quarter. This is all hands on deck. We include six observers from our central office team (three from Instruction, two from Student Services, plus one superintendent), plus the principal and assistant principals. We pair together for the observations, and this allows us to set a standard for what we view as effective instruction. Afterward, we debrief and discuss what went well and what needs to improve for consistency.

If each paired team is able to complete three observations, and we have four teams, twelve observations have taken place, and that is a large slice of any school's instructional program. Principals set the observation schedule purposefully and strategically. Together, we can reach a lot of classrooms!

We use trend data to help determine what professional learning is needed. Notice the circle on the bottom left of Figure 8 that is labeled "Teacher" in the center. Remember the idea of Collective Efficacy? Each of these is intended to help support and move academic achievement forward. The follow-up conversation is often talking about what went well and selecting that one thing that will move the instruction forward.

Our principals meet weekly with our instructional coaches, and they keep a log of their level of impact on learning for teachers (that then moves students). In the next circle, our Professional Learning Communities (PLCs) are one of the next big drivers in achievement, as staff work together to impact learning. Finally, we have SCS University (SCS for Staunton City Schools), our internal professional development program.

Teachers understand that, for each lesson, observers will be looking for a specific learning target, success criteria, and formative assessment. Evaluators look for patterns or trends that are both positive and negative as they relate to education-

The Cycle of Continuous School Improvement
Observations & Feedback
BUILDING TEACHER EXPERTISE
STUDENT GROWTH
The Cycle of Continuous School Improvement
A Layered Model of Instructional Support
Trend Analysis Based on Observation Data
BUILDING ADMINISTRATOR FOCUS
Targeted Professional Learning
BASED ON STRENGTHS/ NEEDS
SYSTEM-WIDE LEARNING
COLLABORATIVE LEARNING
TARGETED SUPPORT
INDIVIDUAL
Teacher
Teacher
OBSERVED CLASSROOM PRACTICE
Observer & Teacher
ONE-ON-ONE FOLLOW-UP CONVERSATION
Instructional Coaching Support
CLASSROOM-BASED COACHING CYCLES
Department / Grade-Level PLCs & Faculty Learning
SHARED REFLECTION AND PROFESSIONAL GROWTH
Division Level PD
DISTRICT WIDE PROFESSIONAL LEARNING

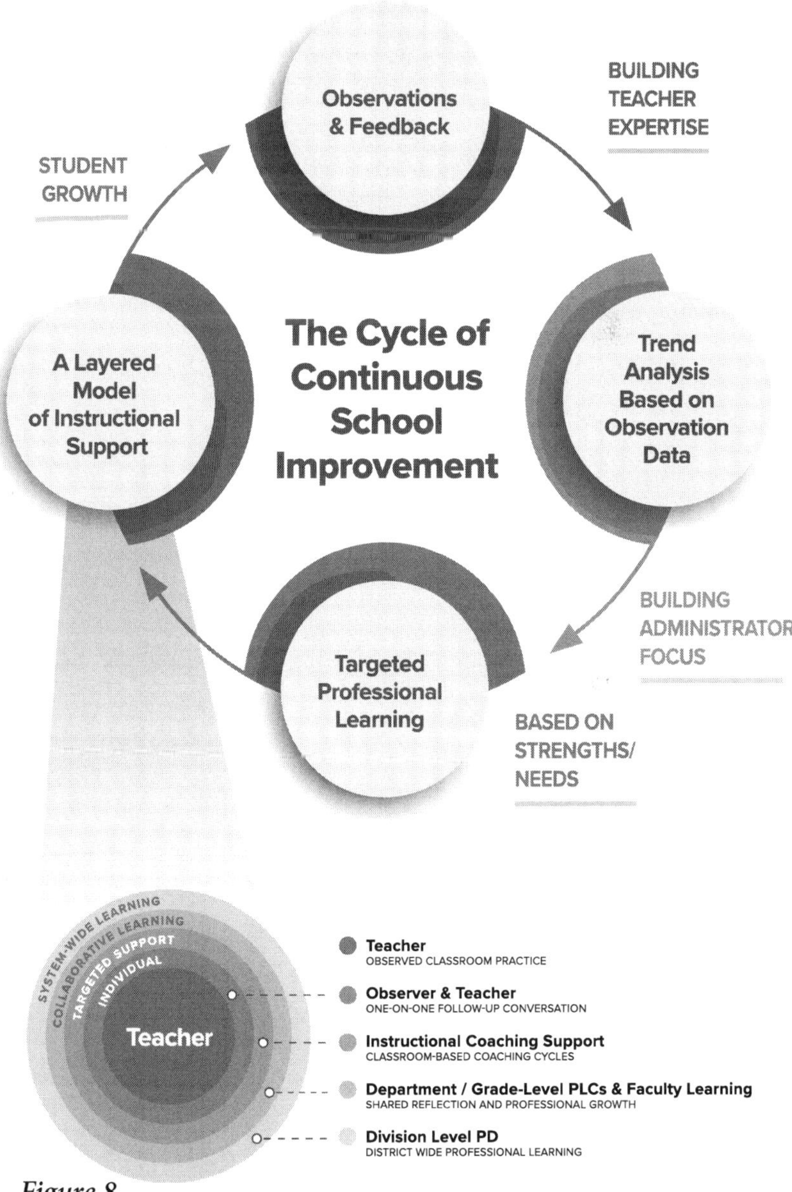

Figure 8

al impact. Both are addressed through targeted professional development.

Feedback is provided at the most individualized level to the whole group level.

Follow-up conversations are for the evaluator and individual teacher.

Instructional coaches can be deployed to an individual teacher or small groups of teachers to address specific trends or to help reinforce what was learned in professional development sessions through a coaching cycle.

Principals, assistant principals, and coaches can provide professional development through PLC meetings or faculty meetings.

Finally, at the division level, problems of instructional practice can be addressed at the organizational level through SCS University.

Our observation and feedback tool works for all grade levels and subject areas.

It doesn't matter if you're observing a high school guitar lesson, third-grade math lesson, or eighth-grade writing lesson. Again, we're looking for the same basic things for each lesson: a learning target and success criteria, the learning activity used to teach the concept, and formative assessment. Then our school leaders are going to provide feedback on what went well (three or less) and even better when (three or less).

No rating scale—just solid feedback!

We observe all teachers, every year. We don't care what year of the evaluation cycle they're on, because that's not what's important. What is important is that school leaders know what's happening in all of their classrooms.

And that they keep going back to the classrooms and teachers that aren't meeting their expectations until they get traction with effective instruction.

How do we know our system works? From 2018 to 2025, Staunton City Schools moved up seventy spots in the academic rankings in Virginia, from 105th to 35th. Over that period, this was the highest level of improvement for any school division in the state.

Figure 9

If your approach to continuous school improvement is working, it shows up in your data.

—GS and SB

CONCLUSION

Project Work and the Problem-Solving Cycle

We hope you enjoyed reading this book, which was written to chronicle our journey through the intertwined themes of compassion, intentional systems, and continuous improvement. We're not quite done with sharing some of our success stories, but first we want to summarize what you've read to this point.

Section One: *Kindness Matters* began with a moment that tested everything we believed about leadership. *Trial by Fire* captured the pain and purpose that emerged from tragedy, and *The Ceremony and the Realization* reminded us that healing and unity can take root in even the most difficult seasons. As we moved through *The Intangibles Surrounding Student Success*, we learned that compassion, connection, and culture are just as vital as curriculum. We had to work to overcome *A Community Divided,* and the *COVID Conundrum* challenged us in ways no one could have predicted. But in response to those things, *The Kindness Challenge* reignited the simple truth that caring for people always comes first. By the time we reached *Full Circle,* we understood that kindness wasn't a soft skill, it was *the* foundation of everything else that worked.

In **Section Two: *ABC Student Success Plans,*** our focus shifted from the heart to the systems that support it. We asked ourselves a hard question in *Why Is It the Same Students, Year After Year?* That question led to *An Idea Is Born,* where the "mad scientist" in each of us began experimenting with ways to support every child in attendance, behavior, and core performance, leading to the ABCs of student success. Through *An Attendance Story, A Behavior Story, A Core Performance Story, A Worker Bee,* and *Cut from a Different Cloth*, we watched students rewrite their own narratives when given the right combination of structure, belief, and opportunity. In *Scaling Up ABC Student Success Plans,* we learned how to turn isolated success into a schoolwide movement, and *The Practitioner's Script* gave us a framework to help other educators bring the same vision to life.

Section Three: *A Cycle of Continuous School Improvement* represented our evolution as leaders. By this point we had seen what was possible when compassion met accountability. In *Practices That Move the Needle* we celebrated the small, consistent actions that produced real change. *The Power of Classroom Presence* reminded us that leaders who show up are visible, engaged, and supportive, and they can shift a school's entire energy. *Beyond the Checklist* invited us to transform observations into meaningful conversations about teaching and learning, and *The Cycle* revealed what we had come to believe most deeply: improvement isn't a program, it's a way of life.

Looking back, our journey wove together three essential truths. Kindness gave our work heart. *Student success planning* gave it structure. Continuous improvement gave it momentum. Together they formed a complete picture of what it means to lead with purpose and teach with impact.

The natural next step in this story was action. In these last pages, we'll take what we've learned and demonstrate how we turned it into purposeful, hands-on project work.

The Power of Projects

Identify a problem of practice. Study it. Eliminate it.

If someone advises you to "think outside the box," they're making the assumption that all possible options inside the

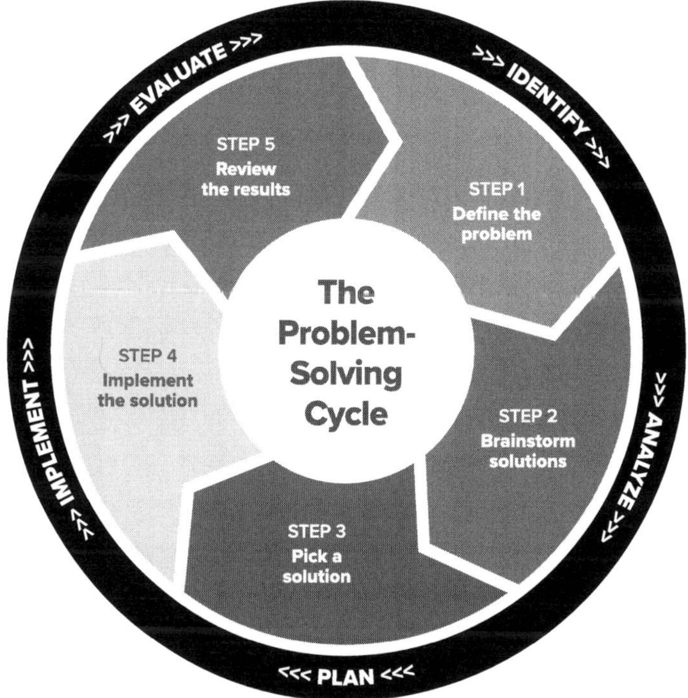

Figure 10

box have already been studied and either eliminated or at least attempted.

That is never the case for schools. There's always a different angle from which to examine a school problem of practice. Let's look at some of those problems.

Bus Driver Shortage

Like other neighboring school divisions, we had a bus driver shortage in 2017–2018. This was causing a lot of stress for families and staff. If we needed to do double runs in the mornings, it caused students to miss valuable instructional time. If we needed to double up bus runs in the evenings, our youngest learners weren't able to be dropped off until after dark.

The situation wasn't acceptable whether you were looking at it through an instructional lens or a student safety lens.

And it wasn't sustainable. We couldn't continue like this in good conscience. We had to figure out a solution.

Our Director of Maintenance, who was also responsible for the Transportation Department, informed me (Dr. Smith) that he had tried just about everything he could think of. He was very connected in our larger school community, but even with those connections, we were still coming up short with drivers.

We had a Chief Financial Officer who operated the budgets on both the city and school sides. It was a huge job, but she managed it expertly. She was a real wizard when came to unlocking financial puzzles. The three of us arranged a meeting to address this urgent problem of practice.

When we looked deeper, we realized that bus drivers were our only employee group *not* eligible for insurance and benefits. Custodians, school nutrition employees, instructional assistants, and every other non-exempt employee did have access to these perks.

Simple question: how could we preach educational equity as an organization and yet be treating one employee group differently than all others?

It was relatively inexpensive to correct the problem of practice in our budget.

Potential candidates came forward quickly upon learning that they could now receive benefits.

The bus driver shortage was eliminated.

Trusted Adult Mentors: Graduation model applied to non- and provisionally licensed teachers

A few years ago at our high school, we had a dedicated team working on a vexing problem of practice. Near the end of the first semester, we had twenty-three seniors in danger of not graduating.

Working with the team on the concept of ABC Student Success Plans and trusted adult mentors, each adult team member selected one, two, or three students with whom they had already established effective working relationships.

I (Dr. Smith) jumped into the work as well by mentoring two of the students since I was fortunate to know them and their families from working in the school division for several years.

We began to meet with students individually, and we ensured that all of their teachers knew what the goal was. Students and staff responded positively. Why? Because they were also at their wit's end trying to figure out how to help students, so they were grateful for the extra support and attention.

Unfortunately, one of my mentees got suspended almost immediately for vaping in the bathroom. I have to admit: I was a little hot.

I called the guardians at home and asked if I could have permission to speak to the student. Again, since I already had a relationship with the family, my request was immediately granted. I let the student know: "Just because you're at home for the next several days, that doesn't mean you can't get your classwork completed."

Our high school principal gathered up the work, and our football coach joined me for a home visit. We sat in the living room and reviewed the assignments with the student while one of his guardians joined the conversation. All three adults delivered a message about our expectation that the student would graduate on time, and we did so in no uncertain terms.

Sometimes, when a student is reluctant to engage, it's helpful to provide perspective. It could go something like this: "Listen, our success is based on your success. When you succeed, we succeed. We're not going to lower our expectations for you, no matter what. But we're also here to support you along the way. We'll all have a good laugh about it after I shake your hand onstage on graduation day."

At the end of the school year at our graduation ceremony, I was able to announce the following to the audience.

"Halfway through the school year, we had twenty-three seniors in danger of not graduating. Our excellent high school team took this problem head-on by assigning each of these students a trusted adult mentor. I'm proud to say that twenty of these students are sitting on this stage right now—and the other three are enrolled in summer school! Our mission is always '100 percent of the students, 100 percent of the time.'"

Prior to the start of each school year, our leadership team would ponder which projects we wanted to tackle. The first step was always identifying an existing problem of practice.

And . . . how urgent is that problem?

Now let's apply what we learned in the graduation model to another problem.

In this era of a nationwide teacher shortage, we were not gaining traction moving our unlicensed or provisionally licensed teachers to full certification. We thought: what if we applied the same model that we used for the high school seniors and graduation last year to our adult staff members?

Working in collaboration with our human resources staff, central office members were assigned a small group of teachers in need of acquiring full licensure.

In effect, each of the adult participants was paired with a trusted adult.

They all now had someone to check in with them regularly and help facilitate the licensure process, which can be very slow, complicated, and frustrating.

At the end of the year, the result was that every teacher made progress, and several achieved full licensure.

A lot of times in schools, it's not the nature of the specific intervention that's most important. It's simply that people—

little ones and big ones—will perform better when they know they have someone in their corner.

Bridging the Digital Divide

From 2012–2017, I (Dr. Smith) had the opportunity to serve with a highly motivated and talented senior leadership team in Newport News Public Schools, led by our visionary superintendent, Dr. Ashby Kilgore. From Ashby and the team I learned about the power of projects for school leaders.

Identify a problem of practice. Study it. Eliminate it.

At the start of the 2019 school year, I was serving as the Staunton City Schools superintendent. We entered into a partnership with T-Mobile for fifty hotspots. We placed twenty-five in both our middle and high school libraries. Families were able to check them out for two weeks at a time.

The partnership was working so well that T-Mobile circled back and said they could now offer several hundred hot spots to the division.

Shortly after that, we were upgrading to new devices for a 1:1 initiative. We asked our team: "What should we do with our old devices?"

If we "recycled" them, we could get about two dollars or three dollars per Chromebook. That didn't seem like a good deal! The first option that we landed on was to offer the used Chromebooks to a neighboring school division. The offer was declined.

The next week, we reassembled the team. Our Director of Technology asked, "What if we could be the first school division in the state to bridge the digital divide?" He had checked with his contacts in the state department, and no division had been able to make that claim.

This was December 2019.

All of our students could use the internet and their Chromebook in school, but it was an equity issue when they left our buildings.

Students without internet access at home were at a distinct disadvantage.

If we paired our hot spots with refurbished Chromebooks, could we actually ensure that every SCS family had internet access and every SCS student had their own Chromebook for home use?

We got to work, using both staff and students, to refurbish the devices. We planned a March rollout to families in need.

Then, in March of 2020, the COVID-19 pandemic hit, and our public schools in Virginia were shut down. Still, we continued our rollout plan.

Families drove to our middle school parking lot where they were handed a hotspot and as many Chromebooks as they needed by school staff wearing masks and gloves. Families were overjoyed, even overwhelmed, upon learning that the Chromebooks were theirs to keep.

Now our school division was better positioned than others to move to a virtual learning model if necessary.

The timing of the rollout with the advent of the pandemic was serendipitous. An operating philosophy in our organizations is this:

If we're working on the right projects for the right reasons, it often turns out to be strategic.

Staff Childcare

The COVID-19 pandemic knocked us all for a loop. But there were strategic lessons learned.

To keep all staff employed during the pandemic, many positions were repurposed. For example, bus drivers became custodians. The cleaning protocols were strict and intensive, so extra help was needed.

Even when our schools were fully virtual, our teachers were required to teach from their classrooms. As a result, several required childcare. Our instructional assistants assumed the important role of being our childcare providers.

The "all hands on deck" approach to teaching and learning during the pandemic brought our employee groups closer together and emphasized that a community of adults working together for the good of our students and community cannot be defeated.

When the pandemic ended, we were able to continue using federal funds to provide free childcare for staff for the next couple of years. Three- and four-year-olds could attend our preschool for free and receive both before and after school care. Kindergarten through sixth grade students of staff were eligible for after school care in each of our three elementary schools. Since our elementary schools have the earliest schedule, before school care was not needed.

As our Elementary and Secondary School Emergency Relief (ESSR) funds neared the end, staff who were utilizing our childcare option were starting to panic.

How could we continue this important program, which seemingly had an exponential effect on developing a positive culture and family feel in our schools and among our staff and students? What lessons could we learn from the pandemic?

We began to have meetings with the city's parks and recreation department, specifically with the director of their HEART program. We brought in our city manager and chief financial officer to discuss how to best continue the program.

We decided that city staff should have the same access to childcare as school staff.

This was a great recruiting tool for our entire city. After a few months of discussion and negotiations, we landed on a cost of $150/month per student for our preschool childcare program, over ten months; and $100/month per student for our after-school program, over ten months.

The city was still able to operate with a small profit at these rates, and they were highly competitive rates in today's childcare market.

High-quality, low-cost childcare options are now in place for both city and school staff, and they continue to this day.

Family Life

At the start of a recent school year, we began to hear from some families that our family life offerings at the middle school level weren't working for their students. We offered a family life section for boys and a separate one for girls.

We were pressed to consider options that weren't gender-specific. This issue is one that always has the potential to be explosive in today's political climate.

At first there didn't appear to be a win-win solution at hand. Then our school board chairperson came up with a novel idea: why not offer three sections of family life?

Our local Office on Youth was able to accommodate this modification. Students and families in our middle schools today have the option of participating in the boys' section, girls' section, or an all-gender section.

A conflict with the potential of having a negative effect on our school culture and community was avoided.

Parental choice was maintained. All students were now included in the program.

The lesson learned? As school leaders faced with seemingly intractable situations, look for a path through the middle. Rather than drawing lines in the sand to stake out a position, do this: listen.

When you're presented with a new idea from stakeholders, don't start with this answer: No. We always need to have a mindset to start with this answer: Maybe. That's when the hard thinking starts. Whether you decide to move forward with the idea or not depends on how it fits with the overall strategic plan. A coherent plan must be maintained to reduce confusion and stress to your school community.

Finally, even if the answer is no, you've modeled respect, listening, contemplation, and follow-through for your stakeholders.

Staff Recognition

What do teachers and staff value?

We could do years-of-service pins, like they do on the city side. But where does that start and end? What do folks do with those years-of-service pins? None of us could even remember what we had done with the pins we had earned in previous school divisions through the years. Maybe in a drawer somewhere?

We could give bonuses. But by the time they're taxed and spread out over twelve pay periods, it doesn't seem like much. Plus, who gets what? And where is the money coming from?

After several weeks of wrestling with this problem in our weekly leadership team meetings, we decided the resource most valued by teachers is . . . time.

We know that well-rested teachers are effective teachers.

The first thing we did was gather input from staff through surveys. Our superintendent/teacher advisory team representatives brought ideas for discussion from their schools. Their input was invaluable.

As a result, we restructured our academic calendar to ensure that teachers have at least one unencumbered work day each month. We extended our Thanksgiving Break to a full week. We committed to ensuring that our Winter Break lasted a full two weeks every year.

We placed two teacher workdays at the start of the second semester in January so teachers could better prepare for the return of their students.

Because we have great belief in the teaching profession, we offered a work-from-home option on select workdays.

Revisiting the academic calendar didn't require any additional funding, just some collaborative thinking and dialogue. The process was intentional because building a sense of camaraderie was an essential outcome. Recognition was achieved because staff felt seen, valued, and heard.

Teachers truly appreciate being treated like professionals. A teacher-friendly calendar, much like staff childcare, became a powerful recruitment and retention tool.

Our Master Plan for school and student success, which we have covered through this book, summed up here.

* * * * *

Are you looking for simple solutions to stubborn school problems? Let's strategize together! See our How to Reach Us page at the end of this book.

—GS and SB

Dr. Garett Smith

Dr. Garett Smith has devoted over 30 years to public education, serving as a teacher, principal, central-office leader, and, since 2017, superintendent of Staunton City Schools. A passionate educator and longtime adjunct professor for the University of Virginia and Old Dominion University, he is widely known for his commitment to equity, high expectations, and meaningful personal connection. Under his leadership, Staunton achieved record academic growth, rising from 105th to 35th in state rankings, posting a 93% graduation rate, closing longstanding achievement gaps, and earning recognition as a top place to work. His tenure has also advanced major initiatives in instructional innovation, student support systems, facilities improvements, and strong community partnerships that support long-term student success. Throughout his career, Dr. Smith has emphasized collaborative leadership, instructional excellence, and the belief that strong schools are built through trust, purpose, and shared responsibility. Dr. Smith holds degrees from the University of Virginia and Marymount University. He and his wife, Wendy, an educator, have two adult children.

For more information on how to reach Dr. Smith, visit

www.gsmithedsolutions.com/services

or scan the QR code below

Dr. Stenette Byrd III

Dr. Stenette Byrd III has built a career spanning more than two decades in public education, serving as a teacher, principal, district leader, and currently as Chief of Schools for Suffolk Public Schools in Suffolk, Virginia. A native of Hampton, Virginia, Dr. Byrd is also an adjunct professor in the School of Education at Old Dominion University and has previously taught at Norfolk State University. He is widely recognized for building strong academic cultures, leading effective school improvement efforts, and providing empowering leadership across diverse educational environments. Throughout his career, Dr. Byrd has guided elementary, middle, and high schools, as well as district-level instructional initiatives, with a focus on student achievement and organizational excellence. He holds degrees from Norfolk State University and Old Dominion University and earned his doctorate in Educational Policy, Planning, and Leadership from The College of William & Mary. He is the proud parent of twins, Stenette IV and Trae Denise Byrd. Dr. Byrd remains deeply committed to mentorship, service, and leadership development.

For more information on how to reach Dr. Byrd, visit
www.thirdforcesolutions.com/services
or scan the QR code below